From the Easy Chair - Volume I

GEORGE WILLIAM CURTIS

Published in 1873

TABLE OF CONTENTS

MOTTO
EDWARD EVERETT IN 1862
AT THE OPERA IN 1864
EMERSON LECTURING
SHOPS AND SHOPPING
MRS GRUNDY AND THE COSMOPOLITAN
DICKENS READING
PHILLIS
THOREAU AND MY LADY CAVALIERE
HONESTUS AT THE CAUCUS
THALBERG AND OTHER PIANISTS 1871
URBS AND RUS
RIP VAN WINKLE
A CHINESE CRITIC
HOLIDAY SAUNTERING
WENDELL PHILLIPS AT HARVARD 1881
EASTER BONNETS
JENNY LIND
THE TOWN
SARAH SHAW RUSSELL
STREET MUSIC
A LITTLE DINNER WITH THACKERAY
CECILIA PLAYING
THE MANNERLESS SEX
ROBERT BROWNING IN FLORENCE
PLAYERS
UNMUSICAL BOXES
THE DINNER IN ARCADIA

MOTTO

"I shall from Time to Time Report and Consider all Matters of what Kind Soever that shall occur to Me." -THE TATLER

EDWARD EVERETT IN 1862

The house was full, and murmurous with the pleasant chat and rustling movement of well-dressed persons of both sexes who waited patiently the coming of the orator, looking at the expanse of stage, which was carpeted, and covered with rows of settees that went backward from the footlights to a landscape of charming freshness of color, that might have been set for the "Maid of Milan" or the pastoral opera. Between the seats and the foot-lights was a broad space, upon which stood a small table and two or three chairs; and if the orator of the evening, like a primo tenore, had been surveying the house through the friendly chinks of the pastoral landscape, he would have felt a warm suffusion of pleasure that his name should be the magic spell to summon an audience so fair, so numerous, and so intelligent.

There were ushers who showed ladies to seats, and with their dress-coats and bright badges looked like a milder Metropolitan police. But no greater force was presumed to be required of them than pressing aside a too discursive crinoline. In the soft, ample light, as the audience sat with fluttering ribbons and bright gems and splendid silks and shawls, so tranquilly expectant, so calmly smiling, so shyly blushing (if, haply, in all that crowd there were a pair of lovers!), it was hard to believe that civil war was wasting the land, and that at the very moment some of those glad hearts were broken--but would not know it until the sad news came. Yet it was easy, in the same glance, to feel that even the terrible shape that we thought we had eluded forever did not seem, after all, so terrible; that even civil war might be shaking the gates and the guests still smile in the chambers.

But while leaning against the wall, under the balcony, the Easy Chair looks around upon the humming throng and thinks of camps far away, and beating drums and wild alarms and sweeping squadrons of battle, there is a sudden hush and a simultaneous glance towards one side of the house, and there, behind the seats at the side, and making for the stage door, marches a procession, two and two, very solemn, very bald, very gray, and in evening dress. They are the invited guests, the honored citizens of Brooklyn, the reverend clergy, and others; a body of substantial, intelligent, decorous persons. They disappear for a moment within the door, and immediately emerge upon the stage with a composed bustle, moving the seats, taking off their coats, sedately interchanging little jests, and finally seating themselves, and gazing at the audience evidently with a feeling of doubt whether the honor of the position compensates for its great disadvantage; for to sit behind an orator is to hear, without seeing, an actor.

The audience is now waiting, both upon the stage and in the boxes, with patient expectation. There is little talking, but a tension of heads towards the stage. The last word is spoken there, the last joke expires; all attention is concentrated upon an expected object. The edge of eagerness is not suffered to turn, but precisely at the right moment a figure with a dark head and another with a gray head are seen at the depth of the stage, advancing through the aisle towards the foot-lights and the audience. They are the president of the society and the orator. The audience applauds. It is not a burst of enthusiasm; it is rather applausive appreciation of acknowledged merit. The gray-headed orator bows gravely and slightly, lays a roll of MS. upon the table, then he and the president seat themselves side by side. For a moment they converse, evidently complimenting the brilliant audience. The orator, also, evidently says that the table is right, that the light is right, that the glass of water is right, and finally that he is ready.

In a few neat words "the honored son of Massachusetts" is introduced, and he rises and moves a few steps forward. Standing for a moment, he bows to the applause. He is dressed entirely in black; wearing a dress-coat, and not a frock. Before he says a word, although it is but a moment, a sudden flash of memory reveals to the attentive Easy Chair all that he has heard and read of the orator before him; how he returned an accomplished scholar from Germany, graced with a delicacy of culture hitherto unknown to our schools; how the youthful professor of Greek at Harvard, transferred to the pulpit of Brattle Street, in Boston, held men and women in thrall by the splendor of his rhetoric and the pleading music of his voice, drawing the young scholars after him, who are now our chief glory and pride; how his Phi Beta Kappa oration in 1824 and its apostrophe to Lafayette, who was present, is still the fond tradition of those who heard it; and how as he passed on from triumph to triumph in his art of oratory, the elegance, the skill, the floridity, the elaboration, the unfailing fitness and severe propriety of his art, with all its minor gifts, consoled Boston that it was not Athens or Rome, and had not heard Demosthenes or Cicero.

If you ventured curiously to question this fond recollection, to ask whether the eloquence was of the heart and soul, or of the mind and lips; whether it were impassioned oratory, burning, resistless, such as we suppose Demosthenes and Patrick Henry poured out; or whether it were polished and skilful declamation--those old listeners were like lovers. They did not know; they did not care. They remembered the magic tone, the witchery of grace, the exuberant rhetoric; they recalled the crowds clustering at his feet, the gusts of emotion that in the church swept over the pews, the thrills of delight that in the hall shook the audience; their own youth was part of it; they saw their own bloom in the flower they remembered, and they could not criticise or compare.

All this recollection flashed through the mind of the Easy Chair before the orator had well opened his lips. The tradition was overpowering. It was not fair, but it was inevitable. If we could see and hear Patrick Henry, with uplifted finger, shouting, "Charles First had his Cromwell, and George Third--may take warning by his example!" would it be, could it be, even with all our expectation, what we believe it to have been? After the tremendous blare of trumpets in advance that shake our very souls within us, no ordinary mortal can satisfy the transcendent anticipation. We lift the leathern curtain of St. Peter's, and catching our breath, look in. Alas! we see plainly the other end of the great church, but with secret disappointment, because we imagined there would be but a dim immensity of space. For the first time we behold Niagara, and resentfully we ask, "Is that all?" The illimitable expectation is too bewildering an overture. So the eyes with which the Easy Chair saw were touched with glamour. The ears with which it heard were full of eloquence beyond that of mortal lips. And there was the orator just beginning to speak. It was not fair; no, it was not fair.

The first words were clearly cut, simply and perfectly articulated. "It is often said that the day for speaking has passed, and that of action has arrived." It was a direct, plain introduction; not a florid exordium. The voice was clear and cold and distinct; not especially musical, not at all magnetic. The orator was incessantly moving; not rushing vehemently forward or stepping defiantly backward, with that quaint planting of the foot, like Beecher; but restlessly changing his place, with smooth and rounded but monotonous movement. The arms and hands moved harmonious with the body, not with especial reference to what was said, but apparently because there must be action. The first part of the discourse was strictly a lucid narrative of events and causes: a compact and calm chapter of our political history by a man as well versed in it as any man in the country; and it culminated in a description of the fall of Sumter. This was an elaborate picture in words of a perfectly neutral tint. There was not a single one which was peculiarly picturesque or vivid; no electric phrase that sent the whole striking scene shuddering home to every hearer; no sudden light of burning epithet, no sad elegiac music. The passage was purely academic. Each word was choice; each detail was finished; it was properly cumulative to its climax; and when that was reached, loud applause followed. It was general, but not enthusiastic. No one could fail to admire the skill with which the sentence was constructed; and so elaborate a piece of workmanship justly challenged high praise. But still--still, do you get any thrill from the most perfect mosaic?

Then followed a caustic and brilliant sketch of the attitude of Virginia in this war. In this part of his discourse the orator was himself an historic personage; for it was to him, when editor of the North American Review, that James Madison wrote his letter explanatory of the Virginia resolutions of '98. The wit that sparkled then in the pages of the Review glittered now along the speech. Here was Junius turned gentleman and transfixing a State with satire. The action of the orator was unchanged. But, in one passage, after describing the wrongs wrought by rebels upon the country, he turned, with upraised hand, to the rows of white-cravated clergymen who sat behind him, and apostrophized them: "Tell me, ministers of the living God, may we not without a breach of Christian charity exclaim,

"'Is there not some hidden curse,
Some chosen thunder in the stores of heaven,
Red with uncommon wrath to blast the man
That seeks his greatness in his country's ruin?'"

This passage was uttered with more force than any in the oration. The orator's hands were clasped and raised; he moved more rapidly across the stage; the words were spoken with artistic energy, and loudly applauded.

Thus far the admirable clearness of statement and perfect propriety of speech, added to the personal prestige which surrounds any man so distinguished as the orator, had secured a well-bred attention. But there was not yet that eager, fixed intentness, sensitive to every tone and shifting humor of the speaker, which shows that he thoroughly possesses and controls the audience. There was none of that charmed silence in which the very heart and soul seem to be listening; and at any moment it would have been easy to go out.

But when leaving the purely historical current the orator struck into some considerations upon the views of our affairs taken by foreign nations, the vivacious skill of his treatment excited a more vital attention. There was a truer interest and a heartier applause. And when still pressing on, but with unchanged action, he glanced at the consequences of a successful rebellion, the audience was, for the first time, really aroused.

Let us suppose, said the orator, that secession is successful, what has been gained? How are the causes of discontent removed? Will the malcontents have seceded because of the non-rendition of fugitive slaves? But how has secession helped it? When, in the happy words of another, Canada has been brought down to the Potomac, do they think their fugitives will be restored? No: not if they came to its banks with the hosts of Pharaoh, and the river ran dry in its bed.

Loud applause here rang through the building.

Or, continued the orator, more vehemently, do they think, in that case, to carry their slaves into territories now free? No, not if the Chief-justice of the United States--and here a volley of applause rattled in, and the orator wiped his forehead--not if the venerable Chief-justice Taney should live yet a century, and issue a Dred Scott decision every day of his life.

Here followed the sincerest applause of the whole evening; and the Easy Chair pinched his neighbor to make sure that all was as it seemed; that these were words actually spoken, and that the orator was Edward Everett.

The hour and a half were passed. The peroration was upon the speaker's tongue, closing with an exhortation to old men and old women, young men and maidens, each in his kind and degree, to come as the waves come when navies are stranded--to come as the winds come when forests are rended--to come with heart and hand, with purse and knitting-needle, with sword and gun, and fight for the Union.

He bowed: the audience clapped for a moment, then rose and bustled out.

--It was not fair; no, it was not fair. The Easy Chair did not find--how could it find?--the charm which those of another day remembered. The oration was an admirable and elaborate address, full of instruction and truth and patriotism, the work of a remarkably accomplished man of great public experience. It was written in the plainest language, and did not contain an obscure word. It was delivered with perfect propriety, with the confidence that comes from the habit of public speaking, and with artistic skill of articulation and emphasis. As an illustration of memory it was remarkable, for it was but the second time that the address had been spoken. It occupied an hour and a half in the delivery, and yet the manuscript lay unopened upon the table. Only three or four times was there any hesitation which reminded the hearer that the speaker was repeating what he had already written. His power in this respect has been often mentioned. He is understood to have said that, if he reads anything once, he can repeat it correctly; but if he has written it out, he can repeat it exactly and always. This unusual facility secures to all his addresses a completeness and finish which very few orators command. He can say exactly what he means, and nothing more, being never betrayed by confusion or sudden emotion to say, as so many speakers say, more than they really think.

But, on the other hand, it is doubtful whether all that electric eloquence by which the hearer is caught up as by a whirlwind and swept onward at the will of the orator, is not now a tradition in the speeches of the orator. The glow of feeling, the rush of rhetoric, the fiery burst of passionate power--the overwhelming impulse which makes senates adjourn and men spring to arms--were they in the orator or in the fascinated youth of those who remember the sermon in Brattle Street, the apostrophe to Lafayette?

AT THE OPERA IN 1864

It was a strange chance that took the Easy Chair, the other evening, to the opera in the midst of a terrible war. But there was the scene, exactly as it used to be. There were the bright rows of pretty women and smiling men; the white and fanciful opera-cloaks; the gay rich dresses; the floating ribbons; the marvellous chevelures; the pearl-gray, the dove, and "tan" gloves, holding the jewelled fans and the beautiful bouquets--the smile, the sparkle, the grace, the superb and irresistible dandyism that we all know so well in the days of golden youth--they were all there, and the warm atmosphere was sweet with the thick odor of heliotrope, the very scent of haute societe.

The house was full: the opera was "Faust," and by one of the exquisite felicities of the stage, the hero, a mild, ineffective gentleman, sang his ditties and passionate bursts in Italian, while the poor Gretchen vowed and rouladed in the German tongue. Certainly nothing is more comical than the careful gravity with which people of the highest civilization look at the absurd incongruities of the stage. After the polyglot love-making, Gretchen goes up steps and enters a house. Presently she opens a window at which she evidently could not appear as she does breast high, without having her feet in the cellar. The Italian Faust rushes, ascends three steps leading to the window, which could not by any possibility appropriately be found there, and reclines his head upon the bosom of the fond maid. We all look on and applaud with "sensation." But ought we not to insist, however, that ladies in the play shall stand upon the floor, and that the floor in a stately mansion shall not be two feet below the front door-sill? And ought we not to demand that Faust shall woo Gretchen in their mother-tongue?

But we, the ludicrous public, who snarl at the carpenter and shoemaker if the fitness of things be not observed; we, the shrewd critics, who pillory the luckless painter who dresses a gentleman of the Restoration in the ruff of James First's court, gaze calmly on the most ridiculous anachronisms and impossibilities, and smite our perfumed gloves in approbation. It is no excuse to say that the whole thing is absurd; that people do not carry on the business of life in song, nor expire in recitative. That is true, but even fairy tales have their consistency. Every part is adapted to every other, and, in the key, the whole is harmonious. Hermann, for instance, the basso, who sang Mephistopheles, would have been quite perfect if he had only remembered this. But he forgot that Mephisto is a sly and subtle devil. He caricatured him. He made him a buffoon and repulsive. Such extravagance could not have imposed upon Faust or Martha; yet we all agreed that it was very fine, and amiably applauded what no opera-goer of sense could seriously approve.

You think that this is taking syllabub seriously, and that the circumstances of the time had made the Easy Chair hypercritical. No; it was only that there comes a time in theatre-going when the boxes are more interesting than the stage. The mimic life fades before the real. In the midst of the finest phrases of the impassioned Herr Faust, what if your truant eyes stray across the parquette and see a slight, pale figure, and recognize one of the bravest and most daring Union generals, whose dashing assaults upon the enemy's works carried dismay and victory day after day? Herr Faust trills on, but you see the sombre field and the desperate battle and the glorious cause. Gretchen musically sighs, but you see the brave boys lying where they fell: you hear the deep, sullen roar of the cannonade; you catch far away through the tumult of war the fierce shout of victory. And there sits the slight, pale figure with eyes languidly fixed upon the stage; his heart musing upon other scenes; himself the unconscious hero of a living drama.

Or, if you choose to lift your eyes, you see that woman with the sweet, fair face, composed, not sad, turned with placid interest towards the loves of Gretchen and Faust. She sees the eager delight of the meeting; she hears the ardent vow; she feels the rapture of the embrace. With placid interest she watches all--she, and the sedate husband by her side. And yet when her eyes wander it is to see a man in the parquette below her on the other side, who, between the acts, rises with the rest and surveys the house, and looks at her as at all the others. At this distance you cannot say if any softer color steals into that placid face; you cannot tell if his survey lingers longer upon her than upon the rest. Yet she was Gretchen once, and he was Faust. There is no moonlight romance, no garden ecstasy, poorly feigned upon the stage, that is not burned with eternal fire into their memories. Night after night they come. They do not especially like this music. They are not infatuated with these singers. They have seats for the season; she with her husband, he in the orchestra chairs. She has a pleasant home and sweet children and a kind mate, and is not unhappy. He is at ease in his fortunes, and content.

They do not come here that they may see each other. They meet elsewhere as all acquaintances meet. They cherish no morbid repining, no sentimental regret. But every night there is an opera, and the theme of every opera is love; and once, ah! once, she was Gretchen and he was Faust.

Do you see? These are three out of the three thousand. There is nothing to distinguish them from the rest. Look at them all, and reflect that all have their history; and that it is known, as this one is known, to some other old Easy Chair, sitting in the parquette and spying round the house. "All the world's a stage, and men and women merely players."

Is it quite so? Are these players? The young pale general there, the placid woman, the man in the orchestra stall, have they been playing only? There are scars upon that young soldier's body; in the most secret drawer of that woman's chamber there is a dry, scentless flower; the man in the orchestra stall could show you a tress of golden hair. If they are players, who is in earnest?

EMERSON LECTURING

Many years ago the Easy Chair used to hear Ralph Waldo Emerson lecture. Perhaps it was in the small Sunday-school room under a country meeting-house, on sparkling winter nights, when all the neighborhood came stamping and chattering to the door in hood and muffler, or ringing in from a few miles away, buried under buffalo-skins. The little, low room was dimly lighted with oil-lamps, and the boys clumped about the stoves in their cowhide boots, and laughed and buzzed and ate apples and peanuts and giggled, and grew suddenly solemn when the grave men and women looked at them. At the desk stood the lecturer and read his manuscript, and all but the boys sat silent and inthralled by the musical spell.

Some of the hearers remembered the speaker as a boy, as a young man. Some wondered what he was talking about. Some thought him very queer. All laughed at the delightful humor or the illustrative anecdote that sparkled for a moment upon the surface of his talk; and some sat inspired with unknown resolves, soaring upon lofty hopes as they heard. A nobler life, a better manhood, a purer purpose wooed every listening soul. It was not argument, nor description, nor appeal. It was wit and wisdom, and hard sense and poetry, and scholarship and music. And when the words were spoken and the lecturer sat down, the Easy Chair sat still and heard the rich cadences lingering in the air, as the young priest's heart throbs with the long vibrations when the organist is gone.

The same speaker had been heard a few years previously in the Masonic Temple in Boston. It was the fashion among the gay to call him transcendental. Grave parents were quoted as saying, "I don't go to hear Mr. Emerson; I don't understand him. But my daughters do." Then came a volume containing the discourses. They were called Essays. Has our literature produced any wiser book?

As the lyceum or lecture system grew, the philosopher whom "my daughters" understood was called to speak. A simplicity of manner that could be called rustic if it were not of a shy, scholarly elegance; perfect composure, clear, clean, crisp sentences; maxims as full of glittering truth as a winter night of stars; an incessant spray of fine fancies like the November shower of meteors; and the same intellectual and moral exaltation, expansion, and aspiration, were the characteristics of all his lectures.

He was never exactly popular, but always gave a tone and flavor to the whole lyceum course, as the lump of ambergris flavors the Sultan's cups of coffee for a year. "We can have him once in three or four seasons," said the committees. But really they had him all the time without knowing it. He was the philosopher Proteus, and he spoke through all the more popular mouths. The speakers were acceptable because they were liberal, and he was the great liberalizer. They were, and they are, the middle-men between him and the public. They watered the nectar, and made it easy to drink.

The Easy Chair heard from time to time of Proteus on the platform--how he was more and more eccentric--how he could not be understood--how abrupt his manner was. But the Chair did not believe that the flame which had once been so pure could ever be dimmer, especially as he recognized its soft lustre on every aspect of life around him.

After many years the opportunity to hear him came again; and although the experiment was dangerous the Chair did not hesitate to try it. The hall was pretty and not too large, and the audience was the best that the country could furnish. Every one came solely to hear the speaker, for it was one lecture in a course of his only. It was pleasant to look around and mark the famous men and the accomplished women gathering quietly in the same city where they used to gather to hear him a quarter of a century before. How much the man who was presently to speak had done for their lives, and their children's, and the country! The power of one man is not easily traced in its channels and details, but it is marked upon the whole. The word "transcendentalism" has long passed by. It has not, perhaps, even yet gone out of fashion to smile at wisdom as visionary, but this particular wise man had been acquitted of being understood by my daughters, and there were rows of "hardheads," "practical people," curious and interesting to contemplate in the audience.

The tall figure entered at a side door, and sat down upon a sofa behind the desk. Age seemed not to have touched him since the evenings in the country Sunday-school room. As he stood at the desk the posture, the figure, the movement, were all unchanged. There was the same rapt introverted glance as he began in a low voice, and for an hour the older tree shook off a ceaseless shower of riper, fairer fruit. The topic was "Table-Talk, or Conversation;" and the lecture was its own most perfect illustration. It was not a sermon, nor an oration, nor an argument; it was the perfection of talk; the talk of a poet, of a philosopher, of a scholar. Its wit was a rapier, smooth, sharp, incisive, delicate, exquisite. The blade was pure as an icicle. You would have sworn that the hilt was diamond. The criticism was humane, lofty, wise, sparkling; the anecdote so choice and apt, and trickling from so many sources, that we seemed to be hearing the best things of the wittiest people. It was altogether delightful, and the audience sat glowing with satisfaction. There was no rhetoric, no gesture, no grimace, no dramatic familiarity and action; but the manner was self-respectful and courteous to the audience, and the tone supremely just and sincere. "He is easily king of us all," whispered an orator.

Yet it was not oratory either in its substance or purpose. It was a statement of what this wise man believed conversation ought to be. Its inevitable influence--the moral of the lecture, dear Lady Flora--was a purification of daily talk, and the general good influence of incisive truth-telling. If we have ever had a greater preacher of that gospel who is he?

SHOPS AND SHOPPING

If the stranger in New York, on any pleasant day, finds himself near Corporal Thompson's Broadway Cottage he will be in the midst of a very pretty scene. Perhaps as he reads these words and asks the question where that romantic cot may be found, he is comfortably seated in it, with his feet placidly reposing upon its window-sills. It is, indeed, in a new form. It no longer looks as it did to the early citizen of fifty years ago, driving out before breakfast upon the Bloomingdale Road, and surveying the calm river from the seclusion of Stryker's Bay. It had an indefinable road-side English air in those far-off mornings. The early citizen would not have been surprised had he heard the horn of the guard merrily winding, and beheld the mail-coach of old England bowling up to the door. There were fields and open spaces about it, for it was on the edge of the city that was already reaching out upon the island. Bloomingdale! 'Twas a lovely name, and 'tis a great pity that the chief association with it is that of a very dusty road.

Meanwhile, if you will contemplate the Fifth Avenue Hotel you will see Corporal Thompson's Broadway Cottage in its present form. But what a busy, brilliant neighborhood it is now! There are shops that recall the prettiest upon the boulevards in Paris; and the people are greatly to be pitied who are too fine to stop and look into them. To be too fine is to lose much. Yet what scion of the golden youth of this moment would dare to walk by the site of Corporal Thompson's Broadway Cottage eating an apple at three o'clock in the afternoon?

There was a grave and well-dressed gentleman who stopped recently at the stand of Mrs. M'Patrick O'Finnigan, which is just in the midst of the gay promenade, to transact some business in peanut candy. The interest of the public in that operation was inconceivable. If he had been Mr. Vanderbilt buying out Mr. Astor--if he had been a lunatic astray from the asylum, or a clown escaped from the circus--he could hardly have excited more attention. The passengers stared in amazement. Some young gentlemen, escorting certain young ladies from school, cracked excellent jokes upon the honest buyer of peanut candy; and if his daughter or any friend had chanced to pass and had seen him, she would probably have been seriously troubled and half ashamed.

Now peanut candy is very good, and at Mrs. M'Patrick O'Finnigan's stand it is very cheap. Nobody is ashamed of liking it, nor of eating it. If the grave gentleman had stepped into Caswell's brilliant shop, let us suppose--where, perhaps, it is also sold--and had called for that particular sweet, nobody would have stared nor made a joke nor felt that it was extraordinary. Yet, how many of the brave generals in the war, who charged in the very face of flaming batteries, would dare to stop at Mrs. O'Finnigan's and buy ten cents' worth of peanut candy if they saw Mrs. Sweller's carriage approaching, or Miss Dasher just coming upon the walk? And as for the Misses Spanker, who daily drive in that superb open wagon with yellow wheels, and who resemble nothing so much as the figures in a Parisian doll-carriage, if they saw an admirer of theirs bargaining for peanut candy at a street stand they would not know him--they would no more bow to a man so lost to all the finer sense of the comme il faut than they would nod to a street-sweeper. It is astonishing what an effect is produced upon some human beings of the tender sex by clothing them in silks cut in a certain form, and seating them in a high wooden box on yellow wheels.

And upon us, also. When the Easy Chair beholds the silken Misses Spanker rolling by, superior, upon those yellow wheels, it is with difficulty that it recalls the cheese and sausage from which all that splendor springs. To-morrow it will be Mrs. O'Finnigan's grandchildren who will look down from their yellow wheels at the peanut and apple stands, and wonder how persons can be so vulgar as to buy candy in the streets. It is a whim of Mrs. Grundy's, who is all whimsey. She will not let us buy a piece of simple candy at the corner, but she will allow us to drag a silk dress over the garbage of the pavement. 'Tis a whimsical sovereign. But we are so carefully trained that it is not easy to disobey her. If to prove your independence you should stop to buy the candy, would the pleasure of asserting yourself balance the unpleasant consciousness that you were wondered at and laughed at?

But the text was shops, and we have drifted into this episode because Mrs. O'Finnigan sells peanut candy in her shop upon the sidewalk near the site of Corporal Thompson's Broadway Cottage, in the midst of the gay spectacle of a summer day. And within a stone's-toss of her stand how many fine houses you will see, and how many other fascinating shops! Our English ancestors were called a shopkeeping nation by Napoleon; but it is his own Frenchmen and Frenchwomen who have the true secret of shopkeeping. They make shops fascinating. They have made shopkeeping a fine art. The other day the Easy Chair stepped into a shop in Maiden Lane, prepared to spend a very pretty sum of money, for a very proper purpose. But if it had invaded the shopkeeper's house, which is his castle, or threatened his hat, which is his crown, it could not have been received more coolly. The disdainful indifference with which its question was answered was exquisitely comical; and the shopkeeper proceeded to look for what was required with a superb carelessness, and an air of utter weariness and disgust of this incessant doing of favors to the most undeserving and insignificant people. It was plainly an act of pure grace that the Easy Chair was not instantly shot into the street as rubbish, or given in charge to the police as a common vagabond.

This worthy attendant--doubtless very estimable in his private capacity--is a serious injury to the business which he is supposed to help. He does not in the least understand his profession. Let an Easy Chair advise him to run over the sea to Paris, and observe how they keep shop in that capital. Does he want a cravat? Here is a houri, neatly dressed, evidently long waiting for him especially, and eager to serve him. "Is it a cravat that Monsieur wishes? Charming! The most ravishing styles are just ready! Is it blue, or this, or that, that Monsieur prefers? Monsieur's taste is perfect. Look! It is a miracle of beauty that he selects. Will he permit?" And before you know it, you foolish fellow, who don't understand the first principle of your calling-- before you know it, she has thrown it around your neck, she has tied it deftly under your chin, and that pretty face is looking into yours, and that pleasant voice is saying, "Nothing could be better. It is the most smiling effect possible!" You might as well hope to escape the sirens, as to go from under those hands without buying that cravat.

This is shopkeeping, and a little study of the art, as thus practised, would be of the utmost service to the Easy Chair's friend in Maiden Lane. The shops there are pretty, and especially during the holidays they are glittering, but they are a little cold and formal. The air of the Boulevards is to be detected only in the neighborhood of Corporal Thompson's Broadway Cottage. Whether cravats are there wafted around the buyer's neck, as it were, entangling him hopelessly in silken and satin webs, the Easy Chair does not know. But it can believe it, as it passes by upon the outside, and beholds the windows which Paris could hardly surpass. Through those windows it sees that, as in Paris, the attendants are often women. It is thereby reminded that in Paris the women are among the most accomplished accountants also; and it remembers that in the same city men are cooks. It is very sure that when Madame Welles, who was afterwards the Marchioness De Lavalette, became at the death of her husband the head of the great banking-house, her cook was a man.

And thereupon the Easy Chair falls into meditation upon "the sphere" of the sexes, and asks itself, as it loiters about the site of the Broadway Cottage, admiring the pretty shops, whether, if it be womanly for woman to keep shop and to acquire property by her faithful industry, it can be manly for man to make laws appropriating and using her property without her consent?

MRS GRUNDY AND THE COSMOPOLITAN

Mrs. Grundy was lately astonished by the remark of a cheerful cosmopolitan whom she proposed to introduce to a very rich man. She seemed to catch her breath as she spoke of his exceeding great riches in the tone of admiring awe which betrays the devout snob. The cosmopolitan listened pleasantly as Mrs. Grundy spoke with the air of proposing to him the greatest of favors and blessings.

"You say he is very rich?" he asked.

"Enormously, fabulously," replied Mrs. Grundy, as if crossing herself.

"Will he give me any of his money?"

Mrs. Grundy gazed blankly at the questioner. "Give you any of his money? What do you mean?"

"Mean?" answered the cheerful cosmopolitan; "my meaning is plain. If I am introduced to a scholar, he gives me something of his scholarship; a traveller gives me experience; a scientific man, information; a musician plays or sings for me; and if you introduce me to a man whose distinction is his riches, I wish to know what advantage I am to gain from his acquaintance, and whether I may expect him to impart to me something of that for which he is distinguished."

Mrs. Grundy, who is easily discomposed by an unexpected turn in the conversation, looked confused, but said, presently, "Why, you will dine with the Midases and the Plutuses." "But they are merely the same thing," said the cosmopolitan, gayly. "You know the story: Mr. and Mrs. MacSycophant, Miss MacSycophant, Miss Imogen MacSycophant, Mr. Plantagenet MacSycophant, Miss Boadicea MacSycophant--and more of the same. One MacSycophant is as good as twenty, Mrs. Grundy; and as I know the Midases already, and find them amusingly dull, why should I know the Plutuses, who are probably even duller?"

Mrs. Grundy looked as if transfixed.

"Oh," continued the cosmopolitan, laughing, "I do not deny that money is an excellent thing. I am glad that I am not in want of it. But it is a dangerous thing to handle. If you don't manage it well it exposes you terribly. Great riches are like an electric light--like a noonday sun; they reveal everything. If a man stands in a ridiculous attitude, or is clad scantily, the intense light displays him remorselessly to every beholder. Great riches do the same. I saw you at the Midases', dear Mrs. Grundy. Did you ever see a more sumptuous entertainment or a more splendid palace? What pictures and statues and vases! what exquisite and costly decoration! what gold and glass! what Sevres and Dresden! But the more I admired the beautiful works of art, the more I thought of the enthusiasm and devotion of the artist, the more I was touched by the grace and delicacy of color and form around me; and the more I heard Midas talk, the more clearly I saw that he did not see, or feel, or understand anything of the real value and significance of his own entourage. The more beautiful it was, the more plainly it displayed his total want of perception of beauty.

"His house is a magnificent museum. It is full of treasures. But they all dwarf and deride him. They are so many relentless lights turned on to show how completely he is not at home in his own house. He is as much out of place among them as a horse in a studio. He has all the proper books of a gentleman's library, and all superbly bound. What does he know about them? He never read a book. He has marvellous pictures. What does he know of pictures? He doesn't know whether Gainsborough was a painter or a potter, or whether Giotto was a Greek or a Roman. He has books and pictures merely because he has money enough to buy them, and because it is understood that a fine house should have a library and a gallery. Is it otherwise with his glass and porcelain? What do you think that he could tell you of Dresden china--its history, its masters, its manufacture? You say that very few people could tell you much about it. Granted; but if a man surrounds himself with it, and forces it upon your attention, you have a right not only to ask such questions, but to expect answers.

"My dear Mrs. Grundy, when I was a young man on my travels, and was introduced at a London club, the porter, or the major-domo, or the door-keeper, or whatever he was, seemed to me like a peer of the realm. He was faultlessly dressed, and he had most tranquil manners. Well, our good friend Midas is that gentleman. He is the curator of a fine museum. He opens the door to a well-furnished club. But he is in no proper sense master of his house. The master of such a house, as Goethe said of the picture-owner, is the man to whom you can say, 'Show me the best.' Poor Midas could only show us the costliest. Eh, Mrs. Grundy?"

That excellent lady's eyes had expanded, during these remarks, until they were fixed in a round, stony stare at the cheerful cosmopolitan.

"And this, you see, my good lady, is the reason that all this display is called vulgar. It represents nothing but money. It does not represent taste, or intelligence, or talent, in the possessor, and the sole relation between him and his possessions is his ability to pay for them. You drink his superior wines. But even you, Mrs. Grundy, are not quite sure that he could distinguish between the finest madeira and a common sherry. That is no fault, surely, but there is a great difference between wines.

"When you kindly offer to present me to a gentleman of whom you can say only that he is very rich, and I ask you if he will give me some of his money, you look surprised and shocked. But I am not a misanthrope, and I ask a question which you can answer affirmatively. He will give me some of his money in giving me some of the pleasure which is derivable from what his money buys. For that I am grateful. I tip the custode with my sincere thanks. I bow to the door-keeper with hearty acknowledgment. I shall go again and again with great pleasure. But I shall not make the singular mistake of supposing that he bears the same relation to his possessions that the musician bears to his music, and the scholar to his knowledge, and the traveller to his shrewd observation.

"You think that I am basely looking a gift horse in the mouth. Not at all. I am only declining to believe the porter to be a peer of the realm merely because he wears a white cravat and has tranquil manners. If Midas is a dull man, all the money in the world does not make him interesting. But if he has accumulated beautiful and interesting things, I shall gladly go to his house and see them. Now, my dear Mrs. Grundy, that is very different from going to his house to see the Plutuses. They are not the possessions that make his house desirable. My young friend Hornet says that if the only way to drink Midas's gold-seal Johannisberger is to take Mrs. Plutus down to dinner, he will not hesitate to pay the price, as he is willing to pay the price of sea-sickness if he wishes to see the Vatican. Does my dear Mrs. Grundy comprehend?"

--But the good lady was gone. She could draw but one conclusion from such a strain of remark about people with fabulous incomes. The cheerful cosmopolitan must have been dining with Mr. Midas, and must have sat much too long at table. What a pity that so pleasant a man should permit himself such excesses! There was, however, but one course for a self-respecting woman to pursue--Mrs. Grundy had left him alone.

DICKENS READING

1867

When, hereafter, some chance traveller picks up this odd number of an old magazine and opens to this very page, let him know that the evening of Dickens's first reading in New York was bright with moonlight veiled in a soft gray snow-cloud. The crowd at the entrance was not large. The speculators in tickets were not troublesome, because all the tickets had been long sold. The police, as usual, were polite and efficient; and going up the steep staircase, and passing through the single door, we were all quietly and pleasantly seated by eight o'clock. The floor of Steinway Hall is level, so that the audience is lost to itself; but it was easy for all of us to perceive, by scanning our neighbors, that we were a very fine body of people. At least everybody who was present said so. We all remarked that the intelligence and distinction of the city were present, and that it must be extremely gratifying to Mr. Dickens to be welcomed by the most intellectual and appreciative audience that could be assembled in New York.

The details of the arrangement upon the platform, the screen behind, the hidden lights above and below, and the stiff little table with the water-bottle, are familiar. But as we all sat looking at them, and at the variously splendid toilets that rustled in, and fluttered, and finally settled, it was not possible to escape the great thought that in a few moments we should see at that queer, stiff table the creator of Sam Weller, and Oliver Twist, and Micawber, and Dick Swiveller, and the rest of the endless, marvellous company--the greatest story-teller since Scott, one of the most famous names in literature since Fielding. When he was here before Carlyle growled in Past and Present about "Schnauspiel, the distinguished novelist," and there were some who laughed. But the laugh has passed by.--Look! There is a man, who looks like somebody's "own man," who scuffles across the stage and turns up a burner or two; and he is scarcely out of the way when-- there he comes, rapidly, in full evening dress, with a heavy watch-chain, and a nosegay in his button-hole, the world's own man.

His reception was sober. The whole audience clapped its gloved hands. Not a heel, not a cane, mingled with the sound, not a solitary voice. It was a very muffled cordiality, an enthusiasm in kid gloves. The Easy Chair, for one, longed to rise and shout. Heaven has given us voices, brethren, with which to welcome and salute our friends, and if ever a long, long cheer should have rung from the heart, it was when the man who has done so much for all of us stood before us. But it was useless. The steady clapping was prolonged, and Dickers stood calmly, bowing easily once or twice, and waiting with the air of one ready to begin business.

The instant there was silence he did begin: "Ladies and gentlemen, I am to have the honor of reading to you this evening the trial-scene from Pickwick, and a Christmas Carol in a prelude and three scenes. Scene first, Marley's Ghost. Marley was dead, to begin with." These words, or words very similar, were spoken in a husky voice, not remarkable in any way, and with the English cadence in articulation, a rising inflection at the end of every few words. They were spoken with perfect simplicity, and the introductory description was read with good sense, and conveyed a fine relish upon the reader's part of the things described. There was nothing formal, no effort of any kind. The left hand held the book, the right hand moved continually, slightly indicating the action described, as of putting on a muffler, or whatever it might be. But the moment Scrooge spoke the drama began.

Every character was individualized by the voice and by a slight change of expression. But the reader stood perfectly still, and the instant transition of the voice from the dramatic to the descriptive tone was unfailing and extraordinary. This was perfection of art. Nor was the evenness of the variety less striking. Every character was indicated with the same felicity. Of course the previous image in the hearer's mind must be considered in estimating the effect. The reader does not create the character, the writer has done that; and now he refreshes it into unwonted vividness, as when a wet sponge is passed over an old picture. Scrooge, and Tiny Tim, and Sam Weller and his wonderful father, and Sergeant Buzfuz, and Justice Stareleigh have an intenser reality and vitality than before. As the reading advances the spell becomes more entrancing. The mind and heart answer instantly to every tone and look of the reader. In a passionate outburst, as in Bob Cratchit's wail for his lost little boy, or in Scrooge's prayer to be allowed to repent, the whole scene lives and throbs before you. And when, in the great trial of Bardell against Pickwick, the thick, fat voice of the elder Weller wheezes from the gallery, "Put it down with a wee, me Lerd, put it down with a wee," you turn to look for the gallery and behold the benevolent parent.

Through all there is a striking sense of reserved power, and of absolute mastery of the art. There is no straining for points, no exaggeration, no extravagance, but an instinctive and adequate outlay of means for every effect, and a complete preservation of personal dignity throughout. The enjoyment is sincere and unique; and when the young gentleman before us remarks to the flossy young woman at his side that "any clever actor can do the thing as well," we congratulate him inwardly upon his experience of the theatre. Perhaps, also, the flossy young woman is of opinion that any clever author can write as well as this reader.

There is a serious drawback to this first evening's enjoyment, however, and that is that fully a third of those present hear very imperfectly. Nothing can surpass the air of mingled indignation, chagrin, and disappointment with which a severe lady just behind declares that she did not hear a word, and adds, caustically, that the spectacle alone is hardly worth the money. Not worth the money? Dear Madam, the Easy Chair would willingly pay more than the price of admission merely to see him. And just as he is thinking so another friend leans forward and says, in a decided tone of utter disappointment, "Just let me take your glass, will you? I can't hear a word, but I should like to see how the man looks." As the Easy Chair passes out of the door he encounters Mr. and Mrs. Sealskin, sailing smoothly and silently out. "How delightful!" exclaims the innocent and unwary Chair. "Didn't hear a word," says Mr. Sealskin, sententiously, and without pausing in his course; and Madam upon his arm raises her eyebrows and looks emphatically "not a word!" So the Easy Chair gradually discovers that there has been a very wide and lamentable disappointment, and that a large part of the throng has been tantalized through the evening in the vain effort to hear--catching a few words and losing the point of the joke. No wonder they are very sober, and sail out of the hall very steadily, with an air of thinking that they have been victims, but also with the plain wish to think as well of Mr. Charles Dickens as circumstances will allow. Still, they evidently hold him, upon the whole, responsible, just as an audience assembled to hear a lecture, and obliged to go unlectured away, holds the lecturer-- chafing in a snow-bank upon the railroad fifty miles away--responsible for its disappointment. It is pleasant for the Sealskins to read, as the Easy Chair did the next morning, in the ever-veracious and independent press, that Mr. Dickens's voice is heard with ease in every part of the hall.

But let them feel as they may, those who did not hear are sure to go again, and if they hear the next time, again and again. Let the future reader of this odd number of a magazine learn further that such was the popular eagerness to attend these readings that people gathered before light to stand in the line of the ticket-office. One historic boy is said to have passed the night in the cold waiting for the opening of the office, and to have sold his prize for thirty dollars in gold to "a Southerner." Another person was offered twenty dollars for his place in the line, with merely a chance of getting a ticket when his turn came at the office.

The interest was unabated to the end, and under the personal spell of the enchanter that old ill-feeling towards the author of American Notes and the creator of Chuzzlewit melted away. And why not? Do we not all know our Yankee brother of whom Dickens told us, who has a huge note of interrogation in each eye, and can we blame the Englishman for using his own eyes? Is not that silent traveller whom he saw still to be seen in every train sucking the great ivory head of his cane and taking it out occasionally and looking at it to see how it is getting on? If we had been a little angry with Lemuel Gulliver or Robinson Crusoe, could our anger have survived hearing one of them tell his story of Liliput, or the other the tale of the solitary island?

After his little winter tour Dickens returned to New York to take leave of the American public. On the Saturday evening before the final reading the newspaper fraternity gave him a dinner at Delmonico's, which was then at the corner of Fifth Avenue and Fourteenth Street, formerly the hospitable house of Moses H. Grinnell. At this dinner Mr. Greeley presided, and that the bland and eccentric teetotaler, who was not supposed to be versed in what Carlyle called the "tea-table proprieties," should take the chair at a dinner to so roistering a blade--within discreet limits--and so skilled an artist of all kinds of beverages as Dickens, was a stroke of extravaganza in his own way. The dinner was in every way memorable and delightful, but the enjoyment was sobered by the illness of the guest from one of the attacks which, as was known soon afterwards, foretold the speedy end. It was, indeed, doubtful if he could appear, but after an hour he came limping slowly into the room on the arm of Mr. Greeley.

In his speech, with great delicacy and feeling, Dickens alluded to some possible misunderstanding, now forever vanished, between him and his hosts, and declared his purpose of publicly recognizing that fact in future editions of his works. His words were greeted with great enthusiasm, and on the following Monday evening he read, at Steinway Hall, for the last time in this country, and sailed on Wednesday. He was still very lame, but he read with unusual vigor, and with deep feeling. As he ended, and slowly limped away, the applause was prodigious, and the whole audience rose and stood waiting. Reaching the steps of the platform he paused, and turned towards the hall; then, after a moment, he came slowly and painfully back again, and with a pale face and evidently profoundly moved, he gazed at the vast audience. The hall was hushed, and in a voice firm, but full of pathos, he spoke a few words of farewell. "I shall never recall you," he said, "as a mere public audience, but rather as a host of personal friends, and ever with the greatest gratitude, tenderness, and consideration. God bless you, and

God bless the land in which I leave you!" The great audience waited respectfully, wistfully watching him as he slowly withdrew. The faithful Dolby, his friend and manager, helped him down the steps. For a moment he turned and looked at the crowded hall. It was full of hearts responding to his own. There was a common consciousness that it was a last parting, and his fervid benediction was silently reciprocated.--Then the door closed behind him.

PHILLIS

There is one lady in literature and in life whom all men are said, not without gentle sarcasm if a woman says it, to wish especially to know. She is declared to be the vision that haunts the youth as his heart opens to the soft influences of love, and her figure, trim and debonair, that allures the older fancy of the man who sits "alone and merry at forty year," having seen his earlier Gillian and Marian and a score more happily married. She is, in fact, the domestic magician, the good fairy, the genius of home, the thoughtful, tactful, careful, intelligent house-keeper, the very she whom Milton sings, introducing us to
"Herbs and other country messes
Which the neat-handed Phillis dresses."
Her name is Phillis--not exactly a romantic name, nor, indeed, is it meant by the poet to be a romantic name; for he has just before sketched another kind of woman:
"Towers and battlements it sees
Bosom'd high in tufted trees,
Where perhaps some beauty lies,
The cynosure of neighboring eyes."
Such a cynosure could not possibly have been named Phillis: Artemis, perhaps, or Hildegarde; Constance, Una, Mildred, or Cunigunda, but by no possibility Phillis. That is a pastoral name, a shepherd's sweetheart. Indeed, the two kinds of women are perfectly indicated and distinguished in these lines of L'Allegro, which have no detail of description. The impression of womanly difference is nowhere more completely given. One picture is that of the lofty, haughty, "highborn Helen," the superb Lady Clara Vere de Vere; the other is that of the thrifty Baucis, the gardener Adam's wife. And the two are as near in the young man's heart as they are in the poem.

When Mr. William Guppy raised his eyes from the pit of the theatre to Miss Esther Summerson sitting in the boxes, the "image imprinted on his 'art" was that of the cynosure of neighboring eyes, stately among stately towers and ancestral trees. But doubtless when Mr. William Guppy, as lovers will, abandoned himself to blissful dreams of the possible home that should grow out of his lofty passion, it was another vision that he saw; it was the high-born Helen coming down to breakfast in a sweet morning-cap, a neat-handed Phillis. For love, which soars and sings, also builds its nest. The one instinct is as deep and sure as the other. The cynosure of worshipping hearts and eyes is but the romantic aspect of Phillis: and because she is so lofty and so lovely will she be the miracle-worker in the household. The secret sorrow of a thousand homes is that the lady of the towers and battlements does not prove in fact to be also the neat-handed Phillis.

Indeed, it is a kind of national complaint and lamentation that the neat-handed Phillis is disappearing altogether. This is the significance of the servant-girl question. This is the root of the alarming conviction that Phillis is changing into Biddy, whose fit epithet is not neat-handed. This is the meaning of the cry for bread--light, sweet, well-baked bread; not the clammy dough which is served to a despairing land. This is the reason of the wondering question, What has become of roast meat? and of the melancholy conviction that henceforth baked beef is to replace the juicy sirloin of tradition, history, and elegant literature.

Of the accomplished and intelligent young women who honor the Easy Chair at this moment with their attention, of course the immense majority can broil a steak to a turn, or mix the airiest bread, or boil potatoes as new-fallen snow. But there are some unfortunates who cannot do it. Let us pity them. They would probably tell us that they have not studied poetry and music, the French language, crochet, and the Boston, to become kitchen drudges: and they will not fail to remind us that Cinderella did not charm the prince as a kitchen-maid, and that she had ceased to be Cinderbreech, and had emerged from the chimney-corner when she married him. But will they please to curb their wrath for a moment and listen to Dr. Clarke? "Unless men and women both have brains, the nation will go down. As much brain is needed to govern a household as to command a ship; as much to guide a family aright as to guide a Congress aright; as much to do the least and the greatest of woman's work as to do the least and the greatest of man's work."

Now, the dressing of messes by the neat-handed Phillis is one of the important elements of governing a household; and the Princess Cinderella was the better housewife because she had once been Cinderbreech. Nelson was the better admiral because he had once been cabin-boy. Dickens was the better story-teller because he had once been reporter. If, indeed, Darby can afford to pay a hundred dollars monthly to a chef, Joan need know nothing of messes; but how many such Darbys are there?

These remarks, or similar ones, have been often heard by the gentler reader, and are somewhat familiar to her, not to say wearisome. "Oh yes," she says, "I know all this: men want women in the family to be angels and French cooks rolled into one. Heaven save the mark! Suppose that women on their side were to expect men in the family to be heroes and gentlemen as well as 'good providers?'"

Well, madame, they ought to expect it and to insist upon it. Perhaps you have played the little game of parlor magic? There are homes in which that game is always played, and they are the happiest of all. In them the real value of neatness and order, of thrift and taste and temperance, is understood, and the Beauty who once lay lapped in lofty towers knows that the romance which enshrined her amid those battlements and tufted trees is preserved and forever refreshed by the art of the neat-handed Phillis. And, madame, upon his side he does not reverse the order of the story and of nature, and sink from the Prince into the Beast.

THOREAU AND MY LADY CAVALIERE

The last time that the Easy Chair saw that remarkable man, Henry Thoreau, he came quietly into Mr. Emerson's study to get a volume of Pliny's letters. Expecting to see no one, and accustomed to attend without distraction to the business in hand, he was as quietly going out, when the host spoke to him, and without surprise, and with unsmiling courtesy, Thoreau greeted his friends. He seated himself, maintaining the same habitual erect posture, which made it seem impossible that he could ever lounge or slouch, and that made Hawthorne speak of him as "cast-iron," and immediately he began to talk in the strain so familiar to his friends. It was a staccato style of speech, every word coming separately and distinctly, as if preserving the same cool isolation in the sentence that the speaker did in society; but the words were singularly apt and choice, and Thoreau had always something to say. His knowledge was original. He was a Fine-ear and a Sharp-eye in the woods and fields; and he added to his knowledge of nature the wisdom of the most ancient times and of the best literature. His manner and matter both reproved trifling, but in the most impersonal manner. It was like the reproof of Pan's statue. There seemed never to be any loosening of the intellectual tension, and a call from Thoreau in the highest sense "meant business."

On the morning of which we are speaking the talk fell upon the Indians, with whom he had a profound sympathy, and of whose life and ways and nature he apparently had an instinctive knowledge. In the slightly contemptuous inference against civilization which his remarks left, rather than in any positively scornful tone, there was something which rather humorously suggested the man who spoke lightly of the equator, but with the difference that there would have been if the light speaking had left a horrible suspicion of that excellent circle. For Thoreau so ingeniously traced our obligations to the aborigines that the claims of civilization for what is really essential palpably dwindled. He dropped all manner of curious and delightful information as he went on, and it was sad to see in the hollow cheek and the large, unnaturally lustrous eye the signs of the disease that very soon removed him from among us. Those who remember him, and were familiar with his truly heroic and virtuous life, or those who perceive in his works that spirit of sweetness and content which made him at the last say that he was as happy to be sick as to be well, will apply to him the words of his own poem in the first number of the Dial:

"Say not that Caesar was victorious,
With toil and strife who stormed the House of Fame;
In other sense this youth was glorious,
Himself a kingdom wheresoe'er he came."

His talk of the Indians left an impression entirely unlike that of the Cooper novel and the red man of the theatre. It was untouched by romance or sentimentality. It made them a grave, manly race, intimately familiar with nature, with a lofty scorn of feebleness. The sylvan shade and the leafy realm and Arden and pastoral poetry were wholly wanting in the picture he drew, quite as much as the theory that they are vermin to be exterminated as fast as possible. He said that the pioneers of civilization, as it is called, among the Indians are purveyors of every kind of mischief. We graft the sound native stock with a sour fruit, then denounce it bitterly and cut it down. What was most admirable in Daniel Boone, he said, was his Indian nature and sympathy; and the least admirable part was his hold, such as it was, upon civilization. He seemed to imply that if Boone could only have succeeded in becoming an Indian altogether, it would have been a truly memorable triumph. Thoreau acknowledged that the Indian was not only doomed, but, as he gravely said, damned, because his enemies were his historians; and he could only say, "Ah, if we lions had painted the picture!"

The sylvan idea of Daniel Boone would probably have been very rudely shattered could he have been actually seen; and Thoreau's Indian was certainly not visible in the stories of men of his time who had passed weeks among the Indians upon the plains. The pioneers, like Boone, are not romantic; their life is a hard toil and struggle; they are ignorant, rude, and even repulsive. This is natural, because their real work is that of the subsoil plough and the harrow. They lay the strong foundations. Without them, no soft waving field of golden harvest, no velvet lawn, no Palladian villa, no flower of art and culture--in a word, no progress, as we call it--however the shade of Thoreau may implacably smile. So when the Lady Cavaliere whispered from under her beaded veil, "Don't speak of it, but I am tired to death of reformers," it was only the artist's impatience of the ploughman; it was Rupert and his men not only sneering at Praise God Bare-bones, and singing their mock prayer in the Lenten litany,

"That it may please thee to suppose
Our actions are as good as those
That gull the people through the nose,"
but heartily believing Cromwell and his men to be canting hypocrites.

And yet the Lady Cavaliere is too well informed not to know that it was not the silken chivalry who planted the king's standard and defended it with all heroism, in whose praise the poets sang, who are still the heroes of romance, and whose life had the charm of grace and ease and accomplishment and savoir faire, that saved England and a great deal more. The lady has sauntered through the palaces where the Vandyck portrait of the king hangs upon the walls, the handsome, melancholy Stuart. She looked at it secretly, perhaps, with something of the same feeling that men think of the hapless Mary, as we call her. What a gentleman! how refined! how sad! how agreeable to the fancy! Yes, dear lady, and what a liar! how false-hearted! who would have had his own foolish way whatever happened to other men! He would have gratified your taste to the utmost; you would never have said under your breath, "How I hate reformers!" he would have, perhaps, carried your imagination and taste against your conscience and judgment. And it is for that very reason--because taste and imagination are so subtly seductive--that it is essential to challenge them. St. Anthony did not mind the devil as a dragon; but the devil as a siren--ah! how hard St. Anthony had to pray!

Change is apt to present itself first in its unhandsome aspect. You would much rather hear a lute in the moonlight upon the lawn, and behold! a coarse plough and a frightful harrow. Yet, so lutes and lawns begin. You like the smooth music of a silken court, the picturesque ceremony, the poetic tradition, the perfume, the splendor, and lo! a troop in jerkin pricking to the fray in horrible earnest, and blood, and ghastly wounds, and torture, and merciful death! Yet, so courts and ceremonies are instituted. One of the hardest battles that reform has to fight is this battle in the air--so to speak: this contest with taste and imagination that cling to the myriad-hued moss and the delicate vine fringe upon the ogre's castle, and that find the donjon so much more picturesque than the house.

A cause is seen through its pioneers, and taste and imagination are confused and confounded in the medium. A nature like Falkland's could not see liberty clearly even through John Pym--how much less through nasal psalm-singing butchers and brewers building a scaffold for the king. So, in our own time, the great question that so sorely rent us was seen by taste and imagination in the form of delicate, highly-cultured women, of a superficial tranquil elegance of society, of patriarchal tradition, of easy knowledge of the world, and the smooth habit of society upon the one hand; and upon the other, often in the form of a queer medley of grotesque people, each more extravagant than the other, and uttering the wildest sentiments in the most absurd rhetoric. The Lady Cavaliere has not forgotten that the last retreat of the doomed system was the salon and the boudoir, where taste is law, and where decorous immorality is not unwelcome.

By-and-by, when the reform is established and has become traditional, its pioneers become heroic and poetic. The Norman robber is then discovered to be a kind of blue-blooded gentleman, or at least the sturdy, aboriginal father of gentlemen. The rough and half-savage Boone is the ideal frontiersman, with a smack of Arden and the sylvan realm. And as for the coarse-toothed harrow--as my Lady Cavaliere sits upon the porch and sees the peacock unfolding his glory upon the soft, thick sward, do you see that my lady wears a delicate trinket around her swan neck, and lo! it is a harrow exquisitely wrought in gold.

The feeling with which she breathed through her beaded veil her dislike of pioneer reformers is as old as human nature. But it was not the sigh of wisdom, but of weariness, in my lady. There is a certain insight even in gentle youth which does not recoil from the pioneer, and foresees the soft sward springing under the harrow as it tears the heavy clods. Those in whom youth abides never outgrow that precious insight and foresight. One such, not less fair than my Lady Cavaliere, of the most tranquil and undemonstrative behavior, has long been to how many good causes one of the most valuable and efficient friends. She has not cared that Daniel Boone should recede into poetic distance before he seemed to her a hero. In his cabin as he smoked, in the hard winter day as he felled the forest tree, in the rough, unhandsome experience of every hour, he has been to her the forerunner of refinement and plenty and ease. If taste and imagination shrink from the squalor of the frontier, she remembers the greater squalor and the darker tragedy of the city slum. If the long-haired, shambling, shrill fanatic upon the platform be a contemptuous jest to my Lady Cavaliere, this fairer lady remembers John clad in goat-skins and crying in the wilderness. I wish, she says, that mankind might sit at a sumptuous table, but I shall not scoff at the wooden spoon that feeds its hunger. She hangs one picture upon her wall: it is Christ sitting at meat with publicans and sinners. And so season after season, year after year, she carries her sympathy, her hope, her steady faith to all the pioneers. She is not a poet, but the world is to her enchanted. Under the sharp voice of the reformer she hears the music of the harmony which he discordantly foretells. With the distorted eyes of the ill-disciplined, ignorant enthusiast she beholds the symmetry of the future towards which he looks. In turn, the reformer and the enthusiast behold in her and vaguely comprehend the outward charm of beauty and grace and high condition which they blindly announce. It is as if Daniel Boone, shaggy and savage, suddenly saw his cabin and his rude clearing glorified: a stately, hospitable mansion, overlooking a placid landscape of rounded groves and blooming gardens and distant parks, murmuring with the song of birds and all domestic sounds. Her service to a good cause is more than eloquence, more than devotion--it is the perpetual presence of its ideal.

There were plenty of Lords and Ladies Cavaliere who were tired to death of that solemn enthusiast and bore, Columbus. But when he saw the shore of San Salvador he must have recalled that he had long ago seen it in the patient faith of any unknown friend who had always hoped for him and believed with him. The Lady Cavaliere who thinks Daniel Boone in early Kentucky, or Christopher Columbus pacing the shore and ceaselessly looking westward, the most romantic of figures, does not know that she sneered at both when she whispered, "I am tired to death of reformers."

HONESTUS AT THE CAUCUS

A man who is easily discouraged, who is not willing to put the good seed out of sight and wait for results, who desponds if he cannot obtain everything at once, and who thinks the human race lost if he is disappointed, will be very unhappy if he persists in taking a part in politics. There is no sphere in which self-deception is easier. A man with a restless personal ambition is very apt to believe his own purposes to be public ends, and he finds his party to be recreant to its principles if he fails to get what he wants. A young man comes from college carefully trained, with the taste for politics which belongs to the English race, and with the wish and hope to distinguish himself and to serve his country. He attaches himself to a party, and works for it in the usual way, waiting for his opportunity and his distinction. Gradually the gratification of his ambition becomes his test of the patriotic sincerity and wisdom of his party. He does not think that it is so. He does not state it to himself in that bald way. But he feels that he is the kind of man that his party ought to promote, that he has the capacity and the desire to be of use, and that if his party has not perceptions sharp enough to know its own best men, nor the wish to distinguish them by calling them to office, there is something deplorable in its condition.

"I am afraid," said a gentleman of this kind to the Easy Chair, "that my party is falling into bad hands. I see signs of corruption which seem to me very disheartening." He shook his head forebodingly. This gentleman did not conceal his opinion. He announced it freely, and the rumor came to the ears of the real managers of the party. They put their heads together, and presently the foreboding gentleman was called to a public position. Again the Easy Chair met him, and he said that the political prospect was very much more encouraging than he had ever known it to be. There was a spirit abroad, he thought, which would certainly lead to great results. Indeed, the clouds were gone, and the sun shone brightly.

At another time another gentleman shook his head in the same way. He held a pleasant position, but he found that promotion was very slow, and he began to despond and to think the times sadly demoralized, and his party--at least he feared it--fatally mercenary. It was evidently indifferent to reform, and seemed to care little for the wishes of the people or the character of the country. He, too, shook his head with profound distrust of the future; and the Easy Chair fell into deep depression, and wondered whether, after all, a republican form of government might not be a failure. Before it was possible to say so conclusively, however, the Chair heard that his friend had decided to seek reform and the welfare of the race "under the banner" of the opposing party. And again, while considering whether all patriots ought not to follow so eminent an example, it learned that the desponding soul who had had the courage to face obloquy and change his party relations had only done so after prolonged and fruitless efforts to secure official place under his old party. Had he obtained it that party would still have seemed to him resolute, patriotic, and discerning, and he would have continued to serve his country in the association to which he had become accustomed.

There is no South American general who overthrows a government and enthrones himself as dictator upon the ruins who does not announce with imposing solemnity that the old system was intolerable, and that the interests of humanity and the country required him to do as he had done. Not one of them was ever known to declare that he had destroyed the old government because he wished to be the government himself. The two friends of the Easy Chair had sincerely sophisticated themselves, and identified their personal advantage and wishes with the public interest. If they had told the precise truth they would have said that they wanted office, and if they could not get it from one party they would try another. When a man is conscious of a strong desire and of great ability to serve the public, this kind of sophistication is easy. That which should make a generous man suspicious under such circumstances is that he confounds official position with public service. The latter, indeed, is in a sense a technical phrase; but a man may equally serve the public unofficially by taking his part in the necessary and disagreeable details of practical politics. If he will not do this he must share the responsibility of bad government.

Yet here, again, he must not be discouraged if his efforts appear to be abortive and the results ridiculous. The secret of a republic seems abstractly to be very simple, for it is merely that all good men shall act together and elect good officers. But good men cannot act together if they do not think together, and the best method of obtaining results which all desire is the very problem of politics. All good men cannot act together, therefore, because good men differ. But even the good men who agree cannot easily and simply have their way, because political measures can be secured only by organization, and the organization, or the machine by which the result is to be attained, may very readily fall into crafty or corrupt hands, which will use the sincerity and pure purpose of better men to serve base and mercenary ends. The first of the two friends of the Easy Chair was used in this manner. He was sincere and pure, but he was vain, and therefore weak, and the clever managers hit him in the heel.

Again, a man may be wholly free of weakness or vanity, and, without the least personal wish or ambition in public life, may take part in politics solely from a commanding sense of duty, and yet find himself and his efforts not only unavailing for his own purposes, but ludicrously and hopelessly perverted to serve those of others. Honestus was such a man: in the truest sense a patriot in feeling, yet he confessed that he had hitherto neglected his political duties, but declared that henceforth he would lose no opportunity of correcting his conduct. He saw with joy the notice of an approaching primary meeting, and when the evening arrived he hastened to the hall with the pleasing consciousness that he was discharging a great public duty. He reached the hall, and was heartily welcomed by the observant managers, whom, had Titbottom's spectacles been at hand, he would have seen to be foxes--at least. They were very glad indeed to see Honestus and men like him engaging in politics. They saw in that fact the augury of a better day. It was a peculiar pleasure to co-operate with him, and they trusted that this was but the beginning of a good habit upon his part. Honestus could not help thinking how easy it was to exaggerate, and to suppose men to be a great deal worse than they are, and wondered that he had never before taken the trouble--or, rather, fulfilled the duty--of attending the primary meeting.

The proceedings began, and he was exceedingly interested. Officers were appointed, and it was evident from their speeches that nothing but honesty and economy was to be sought, and only men of the most spotless character nominated. But it was necessary to have a committee upon nominations; and to his surprise and gratification Honestus heard his own name mentioned as one of the committee, and almost blushed as he was appointed its chairman. The committee was requested to withdraw, and to report the names of candidates as soon as possible.

Honestus and his colleagues therefore retired to a dim passage-way--where, as he subsequently remarked, he should have been rather alarmed to meet either of them at night and alone--and business began. Various names were mentioned, of which, unfortunately, Honestus had never heard one; and at length one of the most positive of the committee said, emphatically, that, upon the whole, Sly was the very man for the place. There was a general murmur of assent and satisfaction. Honestus heard on every side that it was "just the thing;" that Sly was "an A1 boy," and that he was "always there;"

he was also "square," and "right up to the line;" and by common consent Sly seemed to be the Heaven-appointed candidate.

Rather disturbed by his total ignorance of this conspicuous public character, Honestus turned to his neighbor and said, guardedly, with the air of a man who was musing upon Sly's qualifications, "Oh, Sly--Sly?"

"Yes," said his neighbor, "Sly."

"Certainly," replied Honestus; "certainly. But--who--is--Sly?"

His neighbor looked at him for a moment, and repeated the question in a tone of incredulity--"Who is Sly?"--as if he had said, Who is George Washington?

"Yes; I don't think that I know him."

"Don't know Sly?"

"No."

"Well, if you did know him, you'd know that he's just the man we want; bang up; made for it."

"Oh, is he?"

"You bet--A1."

"Well," said the member who had first announced that Sly was the very man for the place, "I suppose they'll be waiting. I nominate Sly as the candidate."

The chairman said yes, but that, unfortunately for himself, he did not know Mr. Sly.

"Well, you don't know anything against him, do you?" asked the other.

"Certainly not."

"Well, we all know him, and he is the very man. We ought to hurry."

Honestus put the question, and Sly was unanimously named as the candidate to be reported to the meeting by the chairman.

The meeting was already stamping and clapping and calling for the committee, and the energetic mover of Sly said that it was necessary to go in right away. The committee made for the hall, and the chairman followed. He knew nothing of Sly nor of the people who had named him, and he knew nobody else whom he could propose for the place. Honestus felt very much as a leaf might feel upon the fall at Niagara, and in the next moment the chairman of the meeting was asking him if the committee were ready to report. The chairman of the committee bowed. The chairman of the meeting said that the report would now be made. Honestus stated that he was instructed to report the name of Sly. The meeting roared. There was some thumping by the chairman, and Honestus heard only the name of Sly and "by acclamation," and a whirlwind of calls upon "Sly!" "Sly!" "Speech!" "Speech!" The next moment Sly, with a large diamond pin, was upon the platform thanking and promising, and the meeting was stormily cheering and adjourning sine die.

Honestus walked quietly home, perceiving that the result of his practical effort to discharge the primary duties of a citizen was that Sly, one of the most disreputable and dishonest of public sharks, had been nominated by a committee of which he was chairman, and that the whole weight of the name of Honestus was thrown upon the side of rascality with a diamond pin. And he reflected that in politics, as elsewhere, it is necessary to begin as early in preparation for action as the rascals.

Yet he did not lose his faith, nor suppose that popular government is a cheat and a snare, because he had been involuntarily made the instrument of knaves. Honestus understands that good government is one of the best things in the world, and he knows that good things of that kind are not cheap. He is willing to pay the price, and the price is the trouble to ascertain who Sly is, and the time to do his part in defeating Sly. For Honestus knows that if he does not rule, Sly will.

THALBERG AND OTHER PIANISTS 1871

It was about fifteen years ago that Thalberg, who has just died only fifty-nine years old, was in this country. Jenny Lind had been here some years earlier, and Alboni and Grisi a little later, and Vieuxtemps and Sivori and Ole Bull a dozen years before. Jullien, with his monster orchestra, had given monstrous concerts in the monstrous hall of Castle Garden, and many a musician of less fame had come to try his fortune. But we had had neither of the acknowledged masters of the piano, the founders of the modern school of playing--Liszt and Thalberg. Liszt, spoiled and capricious, played very seldom. Chopin, more a composer than a performer, we in America had never supposed would cross the sea: so sensitive, so delicate, so shadowy, his life seemed to exhale, a passionate sigh of music. In the stormy, blood-soaked, ruined Paris of to-day it is not easy to imagine those evenings at the Prince Czartoryski's, when Chopin played in the moonlight the mazurkas and polonaises and waltzes which moonlight or dreams seem often to have inspired, but through which the proud movement of the old Polish dance and song triumphantly rings.

In George Sand's Letters of a Traveller Chopin also appears, but sadly and hopelessly. What Xavier de Maistre says of the Fornarina and Raphael is the undertone of all the passages of the book that speak of Chopin--"She loved her love more than her lover." Then came the burial at the Madeleine, with his own funeral march beating time to his grave. The mere pianist who had aroused the most enthusiasm in this country was Leopold de Meyer, who came more than twenty years ago. His was a blithe, exhilarating style. There was a grotesque little plaster cast of him in the shop-windows at the time, representing him crouching over the instrument, with enormous hands spread upon the keyboard, and his fat knees crowding in to cover all the rest of the space. It was slam-bang playing, but so skilful, and with such a tickling melody, that it was irresistibly popular. His "Marche Marocaine," a brilliant tour de force, was always sure to captivate the audience; and his success was indisputable.

De Meyer's concerts were sometimes given in the old Tabernacle in Broadway, near Leonard Street, the circular church which for so many years was the chief public hall in the city. The platform was almost in the centre, and the aisles radiated from it. The galleries went quite around the building, and, except for the huge columns which supported a dome, it was convenient both for hearing and seeing. Here were some of the great antislavery meetings in the hottest days of the agitation. The anniversaries were held here, and it was the scene of all popular lectures and of concerts. A few blocks above, upon Broadway, near Canal Street, was the old Apollo Hall, where the first Philharmonic concerts took place. In those early days of the German music--days which followed the City Hotel epoch and the Garcia opera--people were so unaccustomed to the proprieties of the concert-room that the Easy Chair has even known some persons to whisper and giggle during the performance of the finest symphonies of Beethoven and Mozart, and so excessively rude as to rustle out of the hall before the last piece was ended.

Upon one such occasion it said to its neighbor, as they were coming out:

"It is a pity such ill-mannered people should thrust themselves among ladies and gentlemen."

"Ill-mannered!" quoth its neighbor; "I assure you they are carriage company from the neighborhood of Union Square."

In these days of universal respectful attention at the Philharmonic concerts it is but a curious reminiscence of long-passed boorishness, this of persons who whispered and giggled, and rustled out before the end, at concerts, to the disturbance of all mannerly people.

As the city grew the concerts came up-town, and were for some time given at Niblo's concert-room. But, wherever they were, one person was for many years constantly familiar, sometimes as general director, sometimes as pianist to accompany singing, always modest, courteous, and efficient, a man widely and most kindly remembered--Henry C. Timm. Like most of our musical benefactors, he was a German, and gave lessons in piano-playing. He was not one of the great virtuosos, but his touch was delicate and nimble, and he had a sincere love of his art. Often and often, at a house always pleasant from that reminiscence, with the consent of parent and pupil, and to his own great delight, the hour designed for the scholar's scales and exercises was given to the master's playing. He was fond of Weber's "Invitation to the Waltz," and he played it with force and precision and the utmost delicacy. Mr. Timm had a pale, smooth, sharp face, a rather prim manner, and a quick, modest gait. He was most simple-hearted, and loved a joke; and his fun was all the more effective from his very sober face and his lisp. It was his wife who was long the most efficient actress at Mitchell's old Olympic in the palmy days of burlesque.

It was at Niblo's that Thalberg played. Many of the virtuosos had been--like De Meyer--so extravagant in their action, and so evidently what we now call "sensational," that there was great curiosity to see the master whose name had been familiar since 1830, and famous since 1835, when he first played in Paris. The comparative estimate of the two men, Liszt and Thalberg, was that the former was a player of eccentric genius, the latter of consummate talent: a judgment which is very apt to spring from a superficial theory that eccentricity is the signet of genius. The long hair, the wild aspect of Paganini, did much to confirm this feeling.

At the concerts of Thalberg there were some preliminary performances, and then a gentleman with side whiskers and no mustache, unostentatiously dressed, entered upon the platform. His manner was grave and tranquil, and he bowed respectfully as he seated himself at the instrument. Immediately, without a flourish or grimace, steadily and calmly watching the audience, he touched the piano, and it began to sing. There was no pounding, no muscular contortion. Nothing but his hands seemed to be engaged, and apparently without effort they exhausted the whole force of the instrument. It was in every respect except its great effectiveness the reverse of De Meyer's playing. The effect, indeed, was astonishing. When the player arose, as quietly and gravely as he had seated himself, there was a tumult of applause, to which he bowed and tranquilly withdrew.

The characteristic of his style is well known. It was a series of harmonious combinations of all the resources of the key-board, through which the melody was clearly articulated. It was by study and by long practice only that he carried this method to its perfection. Thus in one of his great fantasias, that from Mozart's "Don Giovanni," the sentiment of the whole opera was reproduced. Perhaps you do not admire brilliant variations upon a theme selected from the opera, but in this performance you are affected by the passionate movement of the entire work. It is a wonderful epitome. The same respect which he showed for his audience and for himself, and which made him always a self-possessed gentleman, he also had for his instrument. De Meyer seemed to suppose that the full range and power of the piano could not be developed except by grotesque methods. Other players treat it as if impatient of its limitations, and resolved to make an orchestra of a feeble key-board. But Thalberg instinctively apprehended the character of the instrument, and respected its limitations as well as its powers, and knew that its utmost resource was attainable by skilled motion rather than by brute force. Therefore he played with his hands, and not with his knees and his body. But the force of his fingers was magical, and the volume of sound that followed was as great as any player evoked.

Thalberg was a player only, and not, in the sense of Chopin, a composer.

What are called his compositions are arrangements and adaptations of themes from operas treated to develop them with all the richness of the instrument. The originality is in the method of instrumentation, and in this he was original, and is really the founder of the present piano school. As a player his characteristic was the cantabile--the singing quality; and this he had beyond all players. The flowing sweetness of his style is indescribable. There were many, indeed, who complained of a want of fire, and denied him that passion without which no work of art is perfect. But it was impossible to hear him play his fantasia from "Don Giovanni," for instance, without perceiving all the passion of the original. Mozart was not lost under his hands. And the impression of coldness was largely due, doubtless, to the tranquillity and propriety of his appearance and manner.

The most generally popular of his successors at the piano in this country was undoubtedly Gottschalk, who was here quite as early as Thalberg, whose fame eclipsed all others. Upon his arrival Gottschalk played privately at a small party. He was a foreign-looking youth, with a peculiarly dull eye, and taciturn, but he was familiar with every kind of music. When he was asked he played Chopin, and with great skill. But his chief successes were his West Indian melodies, which were full of picturesque suggestion. His execution was rapid, brilliant, and forcible, but a great deal of his playing was too evidently tours de force. It was always interesting to watch his audience, when, upon being recalled, he began one of the West Indian strains. There was a minor monotonous theme in them which fascinated the listeners. They heard the beat of the tambourine, and saw the movement of the dance, and with them all the characteristic scenery and association of the tropics filled their imaginations. The languid grace, the rich indolence, the gay profusion of the lands where the banana grows, they felt and saw.

How many admirable players and singers have come among us! And when, as now, one drops through the bridge of Mirza, a host of Easy Chairs pause for a moment to remember how many there were, and to delight in thinking how many more there will be. Once it was the sailor who crossed the sea to find El Dorado and Cathay, now it is the artist who follows in the fascinating quest. But sailor and artist seeking gold in far countries, like the pollen-powdered bee sucking honey in the flowers, bring as rare a treasure as they find.

URBS AND RUS

Mr. Tibs, who has an observing eye for many aspects of life, lately informed the Easy Chair of his conclusion that there are some serious objections to a suburban residence. This is a subject in which so many intelligent and judicious readers of these pages are interested, that the Easy Chair could not be indifferent to Mr. Tibs's conclusions. The population which "sleeps out of town," which goes and comes daily to and from the neighborhood of every great city in every part of the country, is immense and increasing, and it has always rather an air of lofty sympathy and pity for those who still cling to the "sweet seclusion of streets." This is the more observable and amusing because the denizens of town upon their part assume that their fellow-creatures who resort to the country as a residence are mainly impelled by motives of economy. For who would live out of town if he could live comfortably in it?

"You must find it very annoying to be tied to exact hours of trains and boats," says Urbs to Rus, "and it is not the pleasantest thing in the world to be obliged to pick your way through the river streets to the ferry, or wait at stations. However, you probably calculated the waste of time and the trouble before you decided to live in Frogtown."

"Every choice has its inconveniences, undoubtedly," responds Rus, "but I concluded that I preferred fresh air for my children to the atmosphere of sewers and gas factories, and I have a prejudice for breakfasting by sunlight rather than by gas. Then my wife enjoys the singing of birds in the morning more than the cry of the milkman, and the silence at night secures a sweeter sleep than the rattle of the horse-cars. It is true that we have no brick block opposite, and no windows of houses behind commanding our own. But to set off such deprivations there are pleasant hills and wooded slopes and gardens. They are not sidewalks, to be sure, but they satisfy us."

"Yes, yes; I see," says Urbs. "We are more to be pitied than I thought. If we must go out in the evening, we don't have the advantage of stumbling over hummocks and sinking in the mud or dust in the dark; we can only go dry-shod upon clean flagging abundantly lighted. Then we have nothing but Thomas's orchestra and the opera and the bright little theatre to console us for the loss of the frog and tree-toad concert and the tent-circus. Instead of plodding everywhere upon our own feet, which is so pleasant after running round upon them all day in town, we have nothing but cars and stages at hand to carry us to our own doors. I see clearly there are great disadvantages in city life. If a friend and his wife drop in suddenly in the evening or to dine, it is monstrously inconvenient to have an oyster-shop round the corner whence to improvise a supper or a dinner. It would be so much better to have nothing but the village grocery a mile or two away. The advantages are conspicuous. I wonder the entire population of the city doesn't go out to live in Frogtown."

Rus always feels in secret that he is at a disadvantage so long as he must go to town every day to attend to his business. He reasons plausibly that the train or the boat is no more than the horse-car, and he proves conclusively that he can be at his office within half an hour of his friend who lives in Fiftieth Street. But his friend irritatingly replies that on pleasant mornings he prefers not to take the car. He walks down in the bright air and through the busy street. With twinkling and triumphant eyes he invites Rus to do the same.

Rus gayly replies that the sun is quite as bright upon green fields as upon brick blocks or stone flagging, and the shifting panorama from the car window is a lovely picture. Urbs assents, and adds that the dust and cinders also give great zest to the enjoyment, and that dragging through tunnels is full of delight and beauty.

But the real sorrow that Rus feels has not yet been touched. It is the grief which Mr. Tibs has observed and confided to the Easy Chair. It haunts his happy hours with sad foreboding. He cannot look from his window but he sees it. He cannot celebrate the charms of country and suburban life but it seems to mock him. It turns his joy to ashes. He looks upon the wife of his bosom with anguish as he thinks of it. He gazes ruefully into his children's eyes; pretty innocents, they know naught of the impending blow. It is a Shadow, as Thackeray would have solemnly said, with Bulwerian impressiveness, which Pursues Him at Mid Day. It Awakens Him at Mid Night, and Says to Him, Sleep No More! What is it, do you ask? inquires Mr. Tibs, in his most startling manner. Brethren, 'tis the fell hand of improvement. That is it. It is that which harrows the suburban soul and destroys suburban peace. No man who lives in the neighborhood of the city, or in any little settlement, community, hamlet, thorp, village, or town which is occupied with people doing business in the city, but is exposed in his rural retirement, in his suburban home, to the ravages of improvement. There are suburban neighborhoods of New York which are said to be subject to malaria, to fever and ague. It is false, as every denizen of Bay Ridge and Flushing knows. There are others which are alleged to be a prey to mosquitoes and chills. 'Tis a base fabrication, as every Staten Islander and dweller by the Newark marshes is ready to swear. It is notorious, and is established upon the very best authority, namely, that of the inhabitants of the districts themselves, that no shores are so salubrious as those of the bay of New York. Strict justice, indeed, demands--and to nothing so much as strict justice and truthfulness in these matters are the peaceful people of those shores devoted--strict justice and truth demand that it should not be denied that single, exceptional, but upon the whole sufficiently well attested cases of malarial trouble have been known. But they were always brought from abroad, probably from that losel Yankee-land from which most of the woe of New York has proceeded. While, therefore, it is a wanton calumny-- and the corroboration of all suburban property-holders is invited to the statement--to assert that any portion of the neighborhood of New York, or of any other great city, let it be Philadelphia, Chicago, or St. Louis, Boston, Baltimore, or Savannah, is subject to malaria, or is otherwise than the true sanitarium of the continent, yet it must be owned with sorrow that every suburban region is infested with the spirit of improvement.

Edwin and Angelina were married yesterday, and will devote their honeymoon to the quest of a place in which to build their permanent nest. They find it at last in the most delightful of suburban neighborhoods. They build the pretty cottage. They spread out smooth green lawns, and plant trees and shrubs, and hide themselves in flowers. They have made a sweet sylvan seclusion, in which they sit and smile at the eloquence of Urbs, who pities their exile and depicts the charm of streets. Streets are charming, respond Edwin and Angelina in connubial chorus, but we will have none of them. Fond, foolish pair! For even at that moment the desolating spirit of improvement is staking out a street across their most emerald lawn and through their most sacred grove; their trees and flowers and turf are doomed, and their seclusion is to be turned into a dusty highway.

Suburban improvement is the ruthless devastator of home. There is no remedy. To oppose the ruin of the place which you have carefully made, which has grown around you in increasing beauty with the growth and development of your family, which is associated with all that is happiest in your life, and which is in some sort the flowering and expression of yourself, is to be derided as withstanding the public benefit and the advantage of those less fortunate than yourself. The instinct of protecting the home that you have made is denounced as sentimental selfishness, and the law steps forward, cuts down your trees, plows up your lawn, lays a gutter under your window, destroys your home, and hands you some dollars for what it calls compensation, or demands them for what it styles improvement.

I am of opinion, therefore, says Mr. Tibs, and the Easy Chair commends the reflection to those intending matrimony and thinking of a country home, that there are some serious objections to a suburban residence.

RIP VAN WINKLE

Going the other evening to see "Rip Van Winkle," the old question of its moral naturally came up, and Portia warmly asserted that it was shameful to bring young children to see a play in which the exquisite skill of Jefferson threw a glamour upon the sorriest vice.

"See," she said, "the earnest, tearful interest with which these boys and girls near us hang upon the story. The charm to them of the scene and of the acting is indescribable. Do you suppose they can escape the effect? All their sympathy is kindled for the good-natured and good-for-nothing reprobate, and when Gretchen turns him out into the night and the storm, they cannot help feeling that it is she, not he, who has ruined the home, and that the drunken vagabond, who has just made his endearments the cover of deception, is really the victim of a virago. And when he returns, old and decrepit, and, we might hope, purged of that fatal appetite which has worked all the woe, it is his old victim, the woman whose youth his evil habits ruined, and who, in consequence of those habits was driven into the power of the tormentor, Derrick von Beekman, who hands him 'the cup that shall be death in tasting,' as if it were she, and not he, who had been properly chastened and converted from the fatal error of supposing that drunkenness is not a good thing.

"No, no," said Portia, indignantly and eloquently, raising her voice to that degree that the Easy Chair feared to hear the appalling "'sh! 'sh!" of the disturbed neighbors; "it is a grossly immoral spectacle, and the subtler and more fascinating the genius of Mr. Jefferson in the representation, the more deadly is the effect."

The drop had just fallen, and the scene on the mountains was about to open. The house had been darkened, and as the clear, quiet, unforced tone of Rip, yielding, not remonstrating, to the doom that we all knew and he did not, fell upon the hushed audience, the eyes of men and women were full of tears; while the orchestra murmured, mezzo voce, during the storm within and without the house, the tenderly pathetic melody of the "Lorelei:"

"I know not what it presages,
This heart with sadness fraught;
'Tis a tale of the olden ages
That will not from my thought."

It was not easy to find in the emotion of that moment a response to Portia's accusation of gross immorality. There was but a poetic figure in the mind-- the sweet-natured, weak-willed, simple-hearted vagabond of the village and the mountain--touching the heart with pity, and, in the drunken scene, with sorrow. This figure excludes all the rest. Its symmetry and charm are the triumph of the play as acted. Now the immorality can not lie in the kindly feeling for the tippling vagabond, for that is natural and universal. Indeed, the same kind of weakness that leads to a habit of tippling belongs often to the most charming and attractive natures, and the representation of the fact upon the stage is not in itself immoral. The immorality must be found, if anywhere, as Portia insisted, in the charm with which vice is invested.

But is it so invested in this play? It used to be urged against Bulwer's early novels that they made scoundrels fascinating, and that boys after reading them would prefer rascals to honest men. If that had been the fact, the novels would have been justly open to that censure. But, tried by this standard, Rip Van Winkle, as Mr. Jefferson plays it, is far from an immoral play. The picture as he paints it is moral in the same sense that nature is moral. No man, shiftless, idle, and drunken, afraid to go home, ashamed before his children, without self-respect or the regard of others, however gentle and sweet, and however much a favorite with the boys and girls and animals he may be, is a man whose courses those boys will wish to imitate or who will make vice more tasteful to them. The pathos of the second part of the play, in which the change of age mingled with mystery is marvellously portrayed, is largely due to the consciousness that this melancholy end is all due to that woful beginning. The expulsion of Derrick and his nephew is nothing, the happiness of Meenie and her lover is nothing, the release of Gretchen is nothing, there is only a wasted old man, without companions, the long prime of whose life has been lost in unconsciousness, and who, suddenly awaking, looks at us pitifully from the edge of the grave.

By the most prosaic standards this should not seem to adorn vice with attraction. It is true that the spectator is more interested in Rip than in his wife, and that she is made a virago. But it is not his drunkenness that charms, and her virtue is at least severe. Indeed, if this performance is to be tried by this standard, the play must be regarded as a temperance mission. For temperance is to be inculcated upon the youthful spectators who sit near us not so much by stories and pictures of the furious brute who drives wife and children from a home made desolate by him, and who fly from him as from a demon, as by this simple, faithful showing of the kind-hearted loiterer who makes wretched a wife who yet loves him, and who denounces himself to the child that he loves. This is the fair view of it as a picture of ordinary human life.

But, as we look, the low wail of the sad music is in our ears, the scene changes to a weird world of faery, the story merges in a dream, and Rip Van Winkle smiles at us from a realm beyond the diocese of conscience. If conscience, indeed, will obtrude, conscience shall be satisfied. It is a sermon if you will, but if you will, also, it is a poem.

A CHINESE CRITIC

The Easy Chair was agreeably surprised the other day by a call from a
yellowish-visaged gentleman in a queue, who announced himself as of the
family of Lien Chi Altangi, a name which the reader will recall as that of the
Chinese philosopher and citizen of the world whose letters of observation
in England were edited by Dr. Goldsmith. After the natural courtesies of
such a meeting, and the Easy Chair's compliments upon the shrewdness
and charm of his distinguished ancestor's observations, the Chinese
gentleman fell into easy conversation, and was congratulated upon his
singular familiarity with our language. He remarked that it was always an
advantage to a traveller to know the language of the country, and he had no
doubt that so travelling a people as the American were of the same opinion.
"And as you travel over the world more generally than any other people,"
he said, "I presume that you are generally familiar with many languages."
The Easy Chair bowed, and cleared its throat, and smiled, and said, "Oh
yes--probably--undoubtedly."
"Yours is a very great country," the visitor politely returned, "and this city is
indeed magnificent. It promises one day to rival Pekin, at least in extent and
population. The pleasure of seeing your great men--the great men of so
great a city, I mean--must be very unusual, and I should be infinitely your
debtor if you would accompany me to your temple of civic greatness--your
City Hall, as I understand you call it. Your popular institutions, as we are
told in China, are intended to secure worthy governors of the people by the
votes of the people themselves. It is exceedingly interesting, and I am very
anxious to study the working of your institutions in your chief city."
The Easy Chair bowed and cleared its throat again, and answered that the
study of the city was certainly very interesting, but without proffering to
escort the travelling philosopher to the City Hall, it contented itself with

remarking that ours is a very great country, and that its institutions are unequalled in the world.

"I have met no American who is not of that opinion," courteously returned the Chinese gentleman, "and I was pleased to see upon a visit to your Washington and Fulton markets a noble illustration of the generous and becoming manner in which such important parts of your municipal institutions are managed."

The Easy Chair answered that it was not that kind of institution which it had intended by its remark.

"Possibly you allude to another great institution which I have visited," returned the traveller, with exquisite courtesy. "You justly pride yourself upon your advances in sanitary science, and I am a devout pilgrim seeking enlightenment. Judge, then, with what pleasure I saw your chief temple of the customs. What convenience and economy of arrangement! How singularly fitted for its purpose! You are indeed a great people. I passed into the main circular hall, and what purity of atmosphere, what admirable ventilation, what refreshing coolness and sweetness; it is, indeed, a sanitarium; nor can I wonder that you are proud of your progress and achievements in this science. But when I learned that the officers engaged in the public service in this temple, in the business of various accounts, and in determining the value of the products of the whole world, were appointed to the duty because of their zeal in providing candidates for offices and procuring votes for them, I was lost in admiration of institutions under which zealous shouting and running are evidence of skill to embroider muslin and to calculate interest. Truly you are a great people, and your institutions overflow with wisdom."

The Easy Chair bowed and smiled, but the precise terms of an appropriate reply did not suggest themselves, until, remembering what was due to its native land, it began: "There can, however, illustrious son of Lien Chi Altangi, be no doubt that we are a very great and superior people, and that we have a very just pity and contempt for all the unhappy victims of the effete despotisms and hoary empires of the older world--not that we believe the other continents to be actually older, for our own favored continent doubtless emerged first from chaos, but it is an expression which, with the generosity of our institutions, we are willing to tolerate."

"I cannot deny your greatness," politely said the yellowish-visaged gentleman, "and far be it from me to question your superiority. It was but yesterday evening that I attended a social assembly which was described to me as a full-undress party, and as I entered and beheld many of the other sex, I was struck by the accuracy of the description. As I promenaded through the brilliant throng with one of the loveliest of your young persons of that sex, she said to me, with a bewitching smile, 'Dear Mr. Altangi, is it true that Chinese women squeeze their feet for beauty? How very funny!'

"She panted as she spoke, and I saw that her body was evidently incased in some kind of rigid and unyielding garment, and that her waist was surely not the waist of nature. I gazed as intently as decorum would permit--for I am but a student of cities and of men--and I was sure that my lovely companion's body was more cruelly compressed than the feet of my adorable countrywomen, and her panting breath was but evidence of the justice of my observation. I asked her with sympathy if I could not call some companion to relieve her, or, if the case were urgent, whether I could not myself offer succor. But she gazed at me as if I spoke a strange language, and smilingly asked my meaning.

"'Dear miss,' I said, 'are you not in great suffering?' 'Not at all,' she replied, and I paid homage to her heroism. 'I know not, dear miss, whether to admire more the greatness of your heroism or the generosity of your sympathy. While you are in torment yourself, your tender interest goes forth to my countrywomen in what you believe to be torture. Be comforted, dear miss; the anguish of a squeezed foot is not comparable to that of a waist so cruelly confined as yours, and the consequences, also, are not to be compared.' If human bodies in your great and happy country are made like ours in China, certainly, Mr. Easy Chair, I must acknowledge that in heroic endurance of the cruelty of fashion your country is indeed pre-eminent."

There seemed to be such a singular misapprehension upon the part of the courteous visitor that the Easy Chair was beginning again to explain--"Yes, but the indisputable superiority of our glorious country"--when the son of Altangi interrupted, with suavity: "Certainly. I was about to add that while my fair companion insisted that I should confess the pinching of the feet to be a heinous folly, if not, as she was plainly disposed to believe, a crime, my eye was arrested by another lightly and lowly draped figure of the same sex advancing towards us with an uncertain, hobbling step so like the gait of the lovely Chinese maidens of almond eyes that again I watched intently, and I saw that not only was this sylph drawn out of all natural form at the waist, but that she was attempting to walk in little shoes supported upon high pivots called heels under the centre of the feet. It was an ingenious combination of torture and helplessness, to which no social circle in my native land offers a parallel. It is a wonderful achievement, due, I have no doubt, Mr. Easy Chair, to the manifest superiority of your great country, and plainly a striking illustration of it. Yet it is interesting and touching that the maidens of your politer circles, gasping in pinched waists, and balancing and tottering on pivots under their shoes, should inquire with so amused an air about the squeezed feet of Chinese ladies. I pay you my compliments, Mr. Easy Chair, upon your extraordinary country." The urbanity of the visitor was perfect. The Easy Chair looked at his eyes to see if they twinkled, but they had only a bland regard; and as it was beginning again--"Nevertheless, sir, you will admit that the superiority of our institutions"--

there seemed to be so positive an approach to twinkling in the Chinese eyes that the Easy Chair paused, smiled, and then said: "Worthy son of Lien Chi Altangi, thy words enlighten the mind, even as those of thy ancestor illuminated the minds of our fathers over the sea. By their light I read the meaning of the saying that in my youth I heard in the valleys of the Tyrol, 'Beyond the mountains there are men also.'"

HOLIDAY SAUNTERING

The richness and profusion and variety of the Christmas shops in a great city, the sack of the treasures of the whole earth, which furnish such splendid spoil, recall a remark of Buckle. He says that the history of the world shows enormous progress in all kinds of knowledge, in institutions, in commerce and manufactures, and in every pursuit of human activity, but not in knowledge of moral principle. The most ancient wisdom in morals is also the most modern. Time and the progress of civilization have added nothing to the demands of the conscience or to moral perception. The golden rule is an axiom of the most ancient wisdom.

These are bewildering speculations as we stroll along Fourteenth Street and loiter in Twenty-third Street, which, at the holiday season, have especially the aspect of a fair or a fascinating bazaar. The whole world is tributary to Santa Claus.

"Nothing we see but means our good,
As our delight or as our treasure;
The whole is either our cupboard of food
Or cabinet of pleasure."

Invention and science have put a girdle about the globe fitly to decorate Christmas. Diedrich Knickerbocker, in his cocked hat and flowered coat, had heard of Japan, perhaps, as a romance of Prester John. But it would have been a wilder romance for him to imagine his grandchildren dealing at the feast of St. Nicholas with Japanese merchants in Japanese shops upon the soil of his own Manhattan and on the very road to Tappan Zee. Hendrik Hudson might have been reasonably expected to run down from the Catskills with a picked crew to vend Hollands for the great feast. But Cipango--!

Yes; we have subdued distance, we are plucking out even the heart of

Africa. As the streets of Bokhara when the fairs were held were piled with the stuffs of many a province and thronged by merchants of every hue, so the streets of New York at Christmas show that we have taken the whole earth to drop into our Christmas stocking. The festival might be fitly celebrated by coming to the city merely to walk the streets and

"view the manners of the town,
Peruse the traders, gaze upon the buildings."

Happily the eye can appropriate all the treasures that it would be theft for the hand to touch.

Corydon, sauntering with Amaryllis, and staring with her at the wonderful windows, may be a prince by proxy. "Those pearls," he whispers, "the diver plunged into Oman's dark waters to find for you. They are so far on their way, adored Amaryllis. They have reached your eyes, if not yet your ears. Let me but be rich--and I expect at least five dollars for my first fee--let the world but discover that in me the Law, whose seat is the bosom of God, has a new Mansfield, another Marshall, and yonder pearls shall circle the virgin neck for which they were predestined. Or do you prefer the diamonds behind the next pane? Or shall Santa Claus sweetly capture both for you, one for state dress and splendor, one for days less rigorous, not of purple velvets and flowered brocades, but summer draperies of soft lace?"

So the Marchioness and the gay Swiveller, with their happy gift of transforming a shred of lemon-peel and copious libations of pure water into nectar, might have walked the Christmas streets of New York as those of Ormus and of Ind. Lafayette, with the gold snuff-box in which the freedom of the city was presented to him, could not have been freer of it. The happy loiterers could see all the beautiful things, and what could they do more if they should buy them all? Like the kind people at Newport in the summer, who spare no vast expense to build noble houses and lay out exquisite grounds and drive in sumptuous carriages and wear clothes so fine and take pains so costly and elaborate to please the idle loiterer of a day, who gazes from the street-car or the omnibus or the sidewalk, so the good holiday merchants present the enchanting spectacle of their treasures freely to every penniless saunterer, but for the same enjoyment they demand of the rich an enormous price. The poor rich must bear also all the responsibility of possession and care, and cannot be secured against theft or loss.

The splendid streets beguile us from our question. In the brilliant bazaars we are recalling the New York of silence and solitary woods and roving Indians--the New York that the Dutch settlers bought from the Indians for twenty-four dollars, and which is now the city that we behold, the metropolis of the State of which Mr. Draper, its Superintendent of Public Instruction, asks, "Who shall say that these six millions of people are not better housed, better fed, better clothed, more generally educated, more active in affairs, better equipped for self-government than any other entire people numbering six millions, unless it be other citizens of our own country, surrounded by the same circumstances and conditions?" Not the Easy Chair, certainly. On the contrary, it says Amen.

But is Buckle right? Are the six millions as much better morally than the first six millions of their white ancestors upon the continent, as they are better clothed, better educated, and better housed? Are they only materially better? Have they better poets, better artists, than the Greeks, than Dante, than Shakespeare, than Raphael and Michael Angelo? Have they wiser men than Plato, Aristotle, Bacon? Have they higher standards of conduct than those of Confucius and the Hindoos? A hundred years ago the pilgrim was sometimes a week travelling to Albany with great discomfort. To-day we travel thither in three hours with incredible ease and luxury. Do we find more public virtue when we get there? Comfort, knowledge, opportunity, resources, are multiplied a thousandfold. Schools, libraries, museums, societies, appliances, have sprung in a night, like Jack's bean-stalk, to a towering height. Have they brought us nearer heaven? Are we more truthful, more upright, manlier men? In a world where mechanical invention and victories over time and space were of no importance, but where moral qualities alone availed, should we men of the end of the nineteenth century stand any better chance than those of the beginning of the ninth?

That is the queer question which Santa Claus insists upon dropping into the stockings that hang by this Christmas hearth. He calls it a Christmas nut to crack. The old fellow chuckles as he thinks of it while he rides through the frosty starlight. "My children," he laughs, "what is the difference between six dozen dozen and half a dozen dozen?" While he asks and chuckles, the old fellow is himself an answer. He did not invent gifts. But he symbolizes universal giving. The moral law may be as old as man, but the demand and disposition for the general application of that law to actual life increase with every century. The moral law was the same when Howard revealed the horrors of prisons that it is now when modern philanthropy has purged and purified them. "The sense of duty," said Webster, in his greatest criminal argument, "pursues us ever." But it pursues us more effectively with the return of every Christmas.

If there be no larger knowledge of the moral law there is a more universal sense of moral obligation. Those pearls of Oman which Corydon designs for Amaryllis would not have adorned so noble a woman had they circled the neck of the Paphian Venus or Helen of Troy.

WENDELL PHILLIPS AT HARVARD 1881

The great Commencement event of the Summer was Wendell Phillips's oration at the centennial anniversary of the venerable Phi Beta Kappa at Cambridge. It was also the semi-centenary of the orator's graduation at Harvard, and there was great anticipation, not only because Mr. Phillips is now in many ways the first orator of his time, but because his alma mater has not sympathized with his career. On the day before, which was Commencement-day, there was general wonder among the Harvard men of all years whether the orator would regard the amenities of the occasion, and pour out his music and his wit upon some purely literary theme, or seize his venerable mother by the hair, and gracefully twist it out with a smile.

"I hope," uneasily said a distinguished alumnus of Harvard to the Easy Chair, "I hope he will not forget that he is a gentleman."

"He has never yet forgotten it," replied the Easy Chair.

The morning was beautiful--a sweet, fresh, brilliant June morning--and there was a great assembly in the grounds of the university. The usual Phi Beta Kappa attendance is not large. The celebration occurs on the last day of prolonged college festivities, and the number of members of the society is limited; nor, in fact, has it a real existence except on the day of its oration and poem and dinner. This year, however, the centenary of Harvard, from which all the other chapters, except the parent chapter at William and Mary, have proceeded, had drawn delegations from seventeen other colleges. The pink and blue ribbon, which has replaced the square gold watch-key of other days, fluttered at every button-hole, and with pealing music leading the way, the long, long procession--a Phi Beta Kappa procession such as perhaps Harvard never saw before--wound under the imposing buildings towards the beautiful college hall, the Sanders Theatre.

A great college day is always a feast of memory. As the music swelled and the procession moved, the air was full of visions of forms long vanished, of voices forever silent. To the Phi Beta Kappa memory in Cambridge, however, three of the society's famous days returned. First, that 26th of August, 1824, when Edward Everett delivered the oration, which closed with the apostrophe to Lafayette, sitting upon the platform in the old meetinghouse, which stood, we believe, where Gore Hall now stands. It is the college tradition that the audience rose in enthusiasm with the last words of the orator: "Welcome, thrice welcome, to our shores, and whithersoever throughout the limits of the continent your course shall take you, the ear that hears you shall bless you, the eye that sees you shall bear witness to you, and every tongue exclaim with heart-felt joy, Welcome, welcome, Lafayette!" and that Lafayette himself, not clearly apprehending the drift of the peroration, and swept on by sympathy, eagerly applauded with the excited throng. Second, that 31st of August, 1837, when Ralph Waldo Emerson read the remarkable discourse to whose calm, wise, and thrilling words the hearts of men who were young then still vibrate, and to which their lives have responded; and third, the day in 1836 when Oliver Wendell Holmes read his poem, "A Metrical Essay," which is the traditional Phi Beta Kappa poem, as Everett's and Emerson's are the traditional orations. Richard H. Dana, Jr., calls Everett's discourse the first of a kind of which since then there have been brilliant illustrations, the rhetorical, literary, historical, and political essay blended in one, and made captivating by every charm of oratory.

But the procession has reached the theatre, in which already there are ladies seated, and in a few moments the building is filled with an audience to which any orator would be proud to speak. There is music as the audience rustles and murmurs into its place with eager expectation. Then there is a prayer. Then Mr. Choate, the president of the day, with his customary felicity and sparkling banter, speaks of the origin of the ancient and mysterious brotherhood. "And now," he says, in ending, "I introduce to you him who, whenever and wherever he speaks, is the orator of the day." Mr. Phillips rises, and buttons his frock-coat across his white waistcoat as he moves to the front of the platform. Seen from the theatre, his hair is gray, and his face looks older, but there is the same patrician air; and with the familiar tranquillity and colloquial ease he begins to speak.

He spoke perhaps for two hours, perhaps for half an hour. But there was no sense of the lapse of time. His voice was somewhat less strong, but it had all the old force and the old music. He was in constant action, but never vehement, never declamatory in tone, walking often to and fro, every gesture expressive, art perfectly concealing art. It was all melody and grace and magic, all wit and paradox and power. The apt quotation, the fine metaphor, the careful accumulation of intensive epithet to point an audacious and startling assertion, the pathos, the humor. But why try to describe beauty? It was consummate art, and as noble a display of high oratory as any hearer or spectator had known.

It is usually thought that there must be a great occasion for great oratory. Burke and Chatham upon the floor of Parliament plead for America against coercion; Adams and Otis and Patrick Henry in vast popular assemblies fire the colonial heart to resist aggression; Webster lays the corner-stone on Bunker Hill, or in the Senate unmasks secession in the guise of political abstraction; Everett must have the living Lafayette by his side. But here is an orator without an antagonist, with no measure to urge or oppose, whose simple theme upon a literary occasion is the public duty of the scholar. Yet he touches and stirs and inspires every listener; and as he quietly ends his discourse with a stanza of Lowell's that he has quoted a hundred times before, every hearer feels that it is a historic day, and that what he has seen and heard will be one of the traditions of Harvard and of Phi Beta Kappa.

It does not follow, because the audience was charmed, and overflowed with expressions of delight, that it therefore agreed. When an orator calls the French Revolution "the greatest, the most un-mixed, the most unstained and wholly perfect blessing Europe has had in modern times, unless, perhaps, we may possibly except the Reformation," there will be those who differ--who will grant the beneficent results of revolutions, as of wild storms of nature, but who will hesitate to call a movement of which the September days, the noyades, and the bloody fury of a brutal mob were incidents, the most unmixed and the most unstained of blessings. No American would lament the agitation for emancipation, to which the life of the orator has been devoted. It was a great blessing to the country and to humanity; but from the blood of Lovejoy to that of the last victim of the war on either side, it was not an unstained and unmixed blessing. There is, indeed, a sense in which "to gar kings know" that they have a joint in their necks may in itself be called an unstained political gain. But since historically the lesson is taught only by the cruel suffering of the innocent and the guilty together, it is, in fact, indelibly stained. "Ah!" said the most benignant of men, "it was a delightful discourse, but preposterous from beginning to end."

Yet its central idea, that it is the duty of educated men actively to lead the progress of their time, is incontestable. The orator, indeed, virtually arraigned his alma mater for moral hesitation and timidity. But a university lives in its children, and is judged by them; and surely the history of civil and religious liberty in this country from Samuel Adams, James Otis, and Joseph Warren down to Channing and Parker, to Charles Sumner and Wendell Phillips, and the brave boys of whom Memorial Hall is the monument, all of whom were sons of Harvard, does not show that the old university has not contributed her share of leadership.

Such answers, striking and trenchant and admirable, were perhaps made at the delightful dinner which followed the oration. Perhaps President Eliot promptly took up and threw back with eloquent energy the gage which had been thrown in the very face of the venerable mother by one of her eminent children, so illustrating that ample resource and sagacious firmness which have made his administration most efficient and memorable. Perhaps Dr. Holmes, whose felicitous genius overflowing in wit and music has long put the sparkling bead upon the Phi Beta Kappa goblet, recited the lines whose response was the gay laughter that rang through a pelting shower of rain far over the college grounds. Perhaps as "Auld Lang Syne" was sung with locked hands at the end of the dinner, if "Auld Lang Syne" is ever sung at Phi Beta Kappa dinners, there was a general feeling that the day had been a red-letter day for the university, and a white day in the recollection of all who had heard one of the most charming discourses that were ever delivered in the country, and had beheld a display of oratorical art which in this time, at least, cannot be surpassed.

But of all this nothing can ever be known, because the feasts of Phi Beta Kappa are sealed with secrecy.

EASTER BONNETS

It is not a great many years ago that, among Protestants in this country, Easter was mainly the festival of one denomination, and even within that denomination it was celebrated with comparatively little pomp. But now it is universal, especially in the larger towns and cities, and many churches decorate themselves with flowers, and observe with annually accumulating splendor the great feast of the immortal hope. The churches are filled with people. The music is elaborate, and it is elaborately advertised during the preceding week, and, by one of those odd coincidences which associate the most diverse things, it is on Easter-Day that the new spring bonnets of the ladies appear, and there is a delightful mingling of most diverse interests.

"I have observed," said an elderly gentleman, as he watched from the window of his club the pretty procession of new clothes winding churchward on Easter morning, "that some ladies of high fashion dress more and more elaborately as they advance in years, and as the sweet light of youth fades from their eyes it is replaced by a greater blaze of diamonds upon their persons."

It was the venerable Ambassador from Sennaar who spoke, and who was smiling pleasantly upon the cheerful scene.

"For myself," he continued, "I can recall nothing more enchanting in human form than the granddaughter of my old friend whom I went to see some years ago in Newport, and who bounded in at the open window from the garden on a perfect June morning--herself incarnate June--clad in a white muslin dress, her hair simply knotted behind, holding a rose in her hand, and with the loveliest rose in her cheeks. That young woman, a girl not yet twenty, now has girls of her own more than twenty. I wonder if she wears a very elaborate bonnet this Easter morning, and whether her dress is a mass of pleats and puffs and marvellous trimmings, which, when

75

profusely extravagant upon the form of an elder woman, always remind me of signals of distress hung out upon a craft that is drifting far away from the enchanted isles of youth. Is it the instinctive effort to prolong the brilliancy of youth that induces the advancing woman to decorate herself so brightly? Is it the involuntary hope that she will really seem to be buoyant and gay of heart if only her dress be gay? As they go trooping by I mark that richly caparisoned dowager, and I recall the days when I was merely an attache of the embassy, and when in the modest parlor in Bond Street she sang:

"'I wadna walk in silk attire,
Nor siller hae to spare,
Gin I must from my true love part,
Nor think on Donald mair."

The old gentleman from Sennaar is always permitted to have his own way, and he prattles on without interruption. If you don't care to listen, it is always easy to withdraw, and to look out at another window, and to make your own comments instead of heeding his.

"But that was not exactly what I had in mind as I watched this pretty Easter procession," resumed the venerable Ambassador; "but the truth is that when I see a crowd of brightly dressed women, my mind scatters, as it were, and I am very apt not to hit my mark."

The old gentleman smiled again. "All the fine spring bonnets of Easter-Sunday do not prove the youth of every face under them, and I wonder whether this splendid celebration of Easter means that you are a more religious people than in the plainer Easter days that I remember. Is the sincerity of religious feeling always in proportion to the magnificence of the ritual? If it be, you have become a deeply religious people, especially in your great city. We used to think at the legation in Rome that the people of that city were in danger of mistaking a punctual observance of religious ceremonies for religion. But you are so intelligent that you are, of course, in no such danger. I accept these beautiful flowers and this pretty procession of new bonnets as the proof of your religious progress."

The Ambassador paused reflectively a moment, and then continued: "You send a great many missionaries to India and elsewhere. Is it because you have no work for them at home? In my country, my benighted and heathen Sennaar, we have a proverb that an ounce of practice is worth a pound of profession. In Rome, I say, we used to fear lest the people, with crossings and dippings and genuflections and repetitions of a long series of invocations and confessions and penance and many ceremonies, might come to confound these things with religion. But I suppose that this blossoming Easter, this solemn abstention from 'the German' in Lent, and this interest in draperies and postures, mean that you devote the same energy and time and care to studying how to help the helpless, how to console the suffering, how to teach poverty to hope and labor for its own relief. It means that the richly attired Christians who are walking in the most fashionable spring bonnets to church on Easter-Sunday have learned who is their neighbor, and what their duty is towards him, and are diligently doing it."

The Ambassador removed his eyeglasses, and turned to smile blandly upon the group of club-men near him.

"This reflection," he continued, "makes me very happy, and fills me with reverence for a Christian people. For if you built superb churches in one street, and tolerated heathen squalor of soul and body in the next street, you would crucify Christianity. No, no: these sweet flowers of Easter are not symbols of your words, but of your work; not of your professions, but of your practice."

The old gentleman resumed his glasses, and looked silently at the thronged street. How comfortable to believe with our venerable friend, and to perceive that the great increase in the beauty of the Easter commemoration is the fitting symbol of the corresponding increase in our religious faith and practice!

JENNY LIND

It is many years ago that the Easy Chair, making the grand tour, was in Dresden, and saw in the newspaper that Jenny Lind, then in the first fulness of her fame, would sing for four nights in Berlin. It was in the autumn, and loitering along the Elbe and through the Saxon Switzerland was a very fascinating prospect. But the chance of hearing the Swedish Nightingale was more alluring than the Bastei and the lovely view from Konigstein, and at once the order of travel was interrupted, and the Easy Chair arrived eagerly in Berlin.

The Berlin of those days was still a city in which the student could live economically, and hear the lectures of great teachers upon the most reasonable terms. But the sole interest of the moment was the Northern singer, and upon reaching the hotel and making prompt inquiry, the Easy Chair learned that chairs for the Lind representations could be secured only at prices which were wholly unprecedented in the staid Hohenzollern capital. The exigency of the case, however, compelled the payment, and the Easy Chair devoted eighteen thaler, or nearly as many American dollars, to obtaining a seat to hear Jenny Lind for the first time. Never for such a sum was bought so rich a treasure of delightful and unfading recollections, always cheering and inspiring--an unwasting music which has murmured and echoed through a life.

The scene was the Royal Opera-house. The audience was the finest society of the court; and even then the musical taste of Berlin, as if forecasting Wagner, used to sneer loftily at that of Vienna, where Flotow was about to produce "Martha," as a taste for tanzmusik. The opera was the "Sonnambula," and after the pretty opening choruses and dances, Amina came tripping to the front through the clustering villagers.

She was an ideal peasant maiden, blooming and blithe and fair, of an indefinable simplicity and purity; the genuine peasant of the poetic world, not a fine lady of Marie Antoinette's Petit Trianon playing at rustic artlessness. The voice and the singing were but the natural expression of that charming maidenhood. The full volume, the touching sweetness of tone, the exquisite warble, the amazing skill and the marvellous execution, with the perfect ease and repose of consummate art, and the essential womanliness of the whole impression, were indisputable and supreme. To a person sensitive to music and of a certain ardor of temperament there could be no higher pleasure of the kind. Every such person who heard Jenny Lind in her prime, from 1847 to 1852, whether in opera or concert, can recall no greater delight and satisfaction.

Other famous singers charmed that happy time. But Jenny Lind, rivalling their art, went beyond them all in touching the heart with her personality. Certainly no public singer was ever more invested with a halo of domestic purity. When she stood with her hands quietly crossed before her and tranquilly sang "I know that my Redeemer liveth," the lofty fervor of the tone, the rapt exaltation of the woman, with the splendor of the vocalization, made the hearing an event, and left a memory as of a sublime religious function. This explains Jenny Lind's peculiar hold upon the mass of her audiences in this country, who were honest, sober, industrious, moral American men and women, to most of whom the opera was virtually an unknown, if not a forbidden, delight. Malibran had sung here in the freshness of her voice and charm; Caradori-Allan, Cinti-Damoreau, Alboni, Parepa, and other delightful singers followed her. Grisi came, too, but in her decline. Still others have ruled their hour. But in the general memory of the country Jenny Lind remains unequalled. There was the unquestionable quality in her song which made Mendelssohn say that such a musical genius appears but once in a century.

It was a pleasant little New York to which she came, but it thought itself a very important city. Fanny Ellsler had bewitched the town a few years before; and some graybeards and baldheads, now tottering in the sun upon Broadway, but then the golden youth of Manhattan, took the horses from the Bayadere's carriage and drew her in triumph to her hotel. Ole Bull, also, had come conquering out of the North like a young Viking, charming and subduing, and Vieuxtemps came also, disputing the palm. The town took sides. The virtuosi applauded Vieuxtemps as a true artist, and shrugged at Ole Bull as an eccentric player. If you whispered "Paganini?" they silently shrugged the more. Still the young Viking fascinated young and old. He played like the Pied Piper, and the entranced country danced after. But when Jenny Lind came, the welcome to the singer as yet unheard was more prodigious than that offered to any other European visitor except Dickens. It was managed, of course, by Barnum. It was advertising. But that was only until she sang. After that first evening at Castle Garden the delight advertised itself.

In this day, Wagner consule, of the eclipse of Italian opera, the programme of a Lind concert will perhaps win a glance of curiosity even from the lovers of "Tristan und Isolde," who follow with reverence in the parquette the mighty score of the trilogy upon the stage. Here, for instance, is the programme of a charitable concert of Jenny Lind's in Boston on Thursday evening, the both of October, 1850, just a month after her first concert in the country at Castle Garden in New York on the 11th of September. The programme is a pamphlet opening with four marvellous wood-cut likenesses of Jenny Lind, Jules Benedict, her conductor; Signor Belletti, the barytone, and Mr. Barnum. The words or each song in the original and in translation are printed upon separate pages, and the whole concludes with sketches of the lives of Jenny Lind, Signer Benedict, Signor Belletti--and Mr. Barnum. The selection of music comprises Beethoven's overture to "Egmont;" an air from the "Elijah," first time in America, sung by Jenny Lind; "Non piu andrai," from Mozart's "Nozze di Figaro," by Signor Belletti; piano solo, Mendelssohn's "Songs without Words," by Signor Benedict; and, for the first time in America also, "Und ob die Wolke," from "Der Freischutz," by Jenny Lind. This was the first part. The second part began with Reissiger's overture, "Die Felsenmuhle;" Signor Belletti then sang the "Piff Paff," from Meyerbeer's "Huguenots;" Jenny Lind followed with the "Come per me sereno," from the "Sonnambula," for the first time in America; then Belletti with the "Miei rampolli," from Rossini's "Cenerentola;" and the concert ended with the "Dalecarlian Melody" and the "Mountaineer's Song," both for the first time, by Jenny Lind.

It would be still possible even for the devoutest Wagnerian disciple to hear such a concert, perhaps, without leaving the hall in indignation, perhaps even without a protest. All the concerts were of uniform excellence, and the Easy Chair is a competent witness, at least so far as attendance is concerned, for it heard all of the Lind concerts in New York except the first. During the second season an unknown name appeared one evening upon the bill, which announced that Mr. Otto Goldschmidt, a young and unknown pianist, would play for the first time in this country. Tripler Hall, opposite Bond Street upon Broadway, was crowded as usual, and when Jenny Lind had withdrawn after singing one of her "numbers," a slight, dark-haired youth came upon the stage and seated himself at the piano. He was courteously greeted, and just as he was about to begin, the door opened quietly at the back of the stage, and Jenny Lind stood in full view of the audience tranquilly to listen. At a happy point in the performance she clapped heartily, and the whole house, following its lovely leader, burst into a storm of applause. The young man bowed to the audience and to "Miss Lind," and, as he ended, with more hand-clapping and a bright and kindly smile Jenny Lind vanished, having secured the success of Mr. Otto

Goldschmidt. It was a pretty scene. Perhaps the prima donna assoluta recalled the famous brava-a-a-a of Lablache on her first evening at her Majesty's Opera-house in London, which satisfied England that she was a great singer, and confirmed her career. To the audience her friendly interest seemed the impulse of her kindly heart for a young neophyte in this profession. To Mr. Otto Goldschmidt--!

Ole Bull returned to the country before Jenny Lind left it, and one evening, when she was staying at the Stevens House, in Broadway by the Bowling Green, she gave a dinner, and Ole Bull was among the guests. After dinner he seated himself at the piano, and running over the keys, struck into some wild minor chords, and began to sing Norwegian songs. They were of a singular melancholy, but very beautiful, and the company listened intently. Jenny Lind especially sat rapt in the music, until, after one of the songs, she rose quietly, and moving steadily across the floor as if carrying a jar of water upon her head and fearing to spill a drop, she pushed Ole Bull from his chair, and seating herself in his place at the piano, reproduced the entire song with exquisite pathos.

Indeed, it was in these characteristic Northern songs, full of strange and romantic tenderness, and suggestive of solitary seas and wide, lonely horizons, of awful mountain heights and secluded valleys of sober and sequestered life, that her voice seemed most extraordinary and her skill most marvellous. Romantic singing, picturesque, mournful, weird, could go no further. She was the spirit of the North singing its hymn, and the audience sat enchanted under the melodious spell. A veteran, as he recalls those days, might well suspect that he is still enthralled by the magician's wand of youth, and that it is not fact, but only its rosy exaggeration, which he describes. But the contemporary records of that astonishing career remain, and they confirm his story. The prices paid for tickets, the enormous receipts, and the generous gifts in charity of Jenny Lind are not fables. Yet the glamour of youth has its part in all recollection of the days of splendor in the flower. Once when the Easy Chair was extolling the melodious Swede to a senior, the hearer listened patiently, with a remote look in his eyes, and replied at last, musingly, "Yes, but you should have heard Malibran."

The series of American concerts which began on the 11th of September, 1850, at Castle Garden ended at the same place on the 24th of May, 1852. The vast space was not well suited for singing, but the magnificent voice filled it completely, and in the fascinated silence of the immense throng every exquisite note of the singer was heard. She sang with evident feeling, and with responsive tenderness the audience listened. Every time that she appeared she carried a fresh bouquet, the sight of which gladdened some ardent young heart. But when at last she came forward to sing the farewell to America, for which Goldschmidt had composed the music, she bore in her hand a bouquet of white rose-buds, with a Maltese cross of deep carnations in the centre. This she held while for the last time in public she sang in America; and the young traveller who, five years before, had turned aside at Dresden to hear Jenny Lind in Berlin, alone in all that great audience at Castle Garden knew who had sent those flowers.

THE TOWN

In the city that we like to call the metropolis, the newspapers enable us to begin every day with the knowledge that yesterday Mr. and Mrs. A. entertained at dinner Messieurs and Mesdames B., C., D., E., F., G., H., I., and J. And why is this precious knowledge imparted to us? Why are we not also taught what else they did during the day? Why do we learn nothing of Mr. and Mrs. Y. and Z., at the other end of the alphabet, in Baxter Street? For these good folks who are mentioned are in no way distinguished except for riches. If, indeed, they had done or said or written anything memorable, if they had painted fine pictures, or carved statues of mark, or designed noble buildings, or composed beautiful music; if they had effected humane reforms, had happily cheered or refined or enriched human life, or in any way had made the world better and men and women happier, the curiosity to hear of them, and to see them, and to read of their daily course of life, would be as intelligible as the pleasure in seeing the birthplace of Burns, or walking in Anne Hathaway's garden, or hearing of Abraham Lincoln, or seeing Washington's bedstead and sitting in his chair.

But to read day after day in the paper, this golden domesday-book, the lists of rich people who ate terrapin together, or danced together in lace frills and white cravats afterwards, and to read it with avidity, is what might be done in some world of satire. But in a hard-working, sensible, Yankee world! You might say that nobody does read it, but the column of the newspaper which is devoted to this narrative, contrasted with the few paragraphs in which the important news from all parts of the globe is discussed, refutes you. The newspaper understands itself. It is a shrewd merchant who supplies the demand in the market.

But is there no other than a humiliating explanation of the fact? Is it only snobbishness, a mean admiration of mean things? Are we all essentially lackeys who love to wear a livery? Or is it not rather--all this interest in the small performances of those who, if distinguished for nothing else, are the distinguished favorites of fortune--the result of the ceaseless aspiration for a better condition, and the instinct of the imagination to decorate our lives with the vision of a fairer circumstance than our own, and to revenge the tyranny of fate by the hope of heaven? If the fine Titania could sing to Bottom,

"Mine ear is much enamored of thy note,

Thou art as wise as thou art beautiful,"

why should not our liberal fancy sing the same song to the Four Hundred? They may be deftly enchanted to our eyes if to no others, and to our view our Bottom also be translated.

It is not what they are, but what we believe them to be, of which we read in the newspaper. The poor sewing-girl, as she stitches her life away "in poverty, hunger, and dirt," seeing unconsciously the fairy texture and costly delicacy of the robe she fashions, follows it in fancy to the form which is to wear it, and which to that fancy must needs be that of a most lovely and most gracious woman, because none other would that soft splendor of raiment befit. The lofty and benignant lady must needs also mate with her kind, and move only among those "learn'd and fair and good as she." All the circumstance of life must conform, and amid light and perfume and music the unspeakable hours of such women, such men, glide by.--The girl's head droops. For one brief moment she dreams, and that charmed life is real.

In a less degree, in our prosaic and plodding daily routine, we invest the life of the favorites of fortune with an ideal charm. It is, to our fond fancy, all that it might be. Those figures are not what Circe's wand might disclose. They are gods and goddesses feasting, and in happier moments we feign ourselves possible Ixions to be admitted to the celestial banquet. In the streets of the summer city their palaces are closed, their brilliant equipages are gone; they do not sparkle and murmur in their opera boxes, nor roll stately in slow lines along the trimmed avenues of the Park. But still the celestial life proceeds, a little out of sight, its lovely leisure brimmed with deeds becoming those who have no care but to do good and to transfigure their own fair fortune into a blessing for the world. We read the gross details of dress and dinner. But they remind us only more keenly of the ample resource, the boundless opportunity which our favorites of fortune enjoy.

Thus, Orestes, we ponder the society column not because we are snobs, but because our imaginations take fire; the dry narrowness and hard conditions of our lives are soothed as we contemplate those who have no excuse not to be benefactors; and what they should be, our imaginations, benevolent to ourselves, assure us that they are.

SARAH SHAW RUSSELL

There died lately a woman not known to the public, but whose loss to those who personally knew her can never be made good. The summer that shall come may bring as of old roses and violets, but the summer that is gone will never return. In the memory of all of us there are persons who seem to have revealed to us the best that we know and are; they are so lofty that we are raised, so noble that we are ennobled; so pure that we are purified. They are generally women whose lives are noiseless, who live at home, wives and mothers, without the ambition that spurs men to strive for renown, but their days are full of such richness of beautiful life that its fitting image is that finest flower of tropical luxuriance, the magnificent Victoria Regia.

A nature so modest and simple, and a life so private that it seems almost a wrong to speak of them publicly, yet a character so firm and tranquil and self-possessed that if necessary it would have met without doubt or hesitation any form of martyrdom, can hardly be described without apparent exaggeration. She was born, in our familiar phrase, a lady, and from the beginning, throughout a long life, she was surrounded with perfect ease of circumstance. She was singularly beautiful in her youth, and to the close of her life she had the charm of personal loveliness. Her manner was direct and frank and cheerful, and with her perfect candor and vigorous good-sense it scattered the trivial and smirking artificialities of social intercourse as a clear wind from the north-west cools and refreshes the sultry languors of August. Early married to a man of the highest character and aims, and of that practical good-sense which makes ability most effective, she was in entire sympathy with his wise and humane interests, and thus in her family she was most fortunate and happy.

Yet by beauty, wealth, position, and the natural possession of the prizes for which life is generally a struggle, she was wholly unspoiled. Her views of duty and of just human relations were so clear and true that she reinvigorated the conscience of all who knew her. She was curiously free from the little weaknesses which we instinctively excuse in ourselves and others, and although her absolute truthfulness necessarily but involuntarily rebuked us all, we could no more be angry than with our own consciences. The reproach was entirely involuntary. Never was a woman more tenderly tolerant of every honest difference, or more careful not to wound either by look or word or tone. Too true herself to suspect falsity in others, she was much too sensible to assume the part of Mentor.

In the great mental and moral activity of her generation she was instinctively liberal, and never questioned in others the complete soul-liberty, as Roger Williams called it, which she calmly and naturally maintained for herself. No reform could conceal from her its essential value as a high aspiration, a good impulse, if nothing more; and however grotesque and extravagant the reformer, she pierced his mask of eccentricity and welcomed the earnest seeker, bewildered and blinded though he might be. She judged speech and action by a remarkable intuition of right and wrong, and it was interesting to see how surely and smoothly she cut sophistry straight through to the truth which it muffled and distorted. Men and women she valued solely for their intrinsic worth, and never by conventional standards. A fugitive slave and the Prince of Wales would have been treated by her in a way which would have assured them both that the different circumstances of their condition did not obscure their equal humanity.

To say this must not leave the impression that she was other than a lady of the simplest, most refined, and most unobtrusive but cordial manner. There must be no vision of a Lady Bountiful, or of a Lady of the Manor, or of any self-conscious personage whatever. But a stronger influence upon the lives with which she was brought in contact cannot well be conceived, nor the perennial hope and encouragement which her cheerful presence inspired. Domestic sorrows touched that strong and noble heart not to any vehement demonstration, but to a deeper faith and a sober serenity, which interpreted the poet's sense of "the still sad music of humanity." Courage, confidence, cheerfulness--these were the good angels that dwelt with her, and through her they breathed their benediction on all whom she loved or who personally knew her. As she lived in communion with great thoughts and the widest human sympathies, so that her life, like our stillest, harvest-ripening days, passed in sunny repose, so the end was peace. With no wasting malady, no long decay of faculty, she tranquilly slept.

There is nothing that poets feign of women that was not justified by her. In thinking of her lofty life there is no need of excuse or allowance; for human nature, as it was never more unassuming or simple, was never greater and lovelier than in her. Beautiful and wise and brave and gentle and good, the thought of her is perpetual blessing.

STREET MUSIC

A man grinding a hand-organ in the street is doubtless a sturdy beggar soliciting alms. A band of men blowing simultaneously into brass instruments, with a brazen pretence of making music, is probably like steam-whistles and church-bells and the cries of newspaper extras and of itinerant peddlers of many wares--a noisy nuisance. Yet the old cries of London, although doubtless strident and disturbing, have a certain romantic charm of association and tradition. Like the Tower and Billingsgate and Wapping Old Stairs, they were parts of very London, and London was less London when they ceased.

Were those old cries of the story-book, like the interpreted voices of the church-bells--

"Kettles and pans,
Says the bell of St. Ann's;
Apples and lemons,
Says the bell of St. Clement's,"--

altogether shameless and exasperating noises? Were they not the same voices that called Whittington to turn again? Was not the deep bay of St. Paul's heard when Nelson, the old sea-dog, died? Could the music of the bells be spared from the story of London more than that of the cries? Is the milkman who announces the arrival of the morning's milk with a "barbaric yawp," like that in which Mr. Whitman is supposed to celebrate his own personality, a sturdy beggar? He would certainly resent the imputation. He is a merchant who sells a desirable commodity. Shall he be adjudged a nuisance?

But Signor Raffaello da Perugia, who produces opera airs upon a portable organ, with Don Whiskerando, who mounts with agility to the parlor window to receive the consideration in his feathered cap, is he not also a merchant who sells music to you in selected varieties, the latest popular songs and tunes of the theatre, the waltz of last year's ball-room? Must he be accounted a sturdy beggar because you happen not to be in immediate want of his wares? Or the band of which we were speaking, which arrives at the hour when the master of the house returns from his office, and performs a serenade of welcome as he greets the circle from which he has been absent since breakfast, shall it be denied the pleasure of heightening the pleasure of others? Are not the taxes of these Jem Baggses, these wandering minstrels, the "only rates uninvidious in the levy, ungrudged in the assessment?"

Where the intent is so unequivocally kindly, is it not gross and unfeeling to suggest in the modest orchestra a questionable chord, a cracked reed, a cornet out of tune? Why so insistent, so scrupulously exigent? Are you never out of tune, good sir? Your chords, say in the domestic concert, are they always finely harmonious, and your own reed never cracked? Why so eager to cast the first stone? Yonder trombone may have its weaknesses-- who of us, pray, is without? Has tolerance gone out with astrology? "He had his faults," said the Reverend Bland Sudds yesterday in a funeral discourse upon the Honorable Richard Turpin--"he had his faults, yes, for he was human." But if a man may falter, shall we not forgive to a trombone even a half-note? If Turpin may be respectfully lamented with indulgent hope, shall a hesitating horn be doomed to "the all-sweeping besom of societarian reformation?"

While Eugenio was making the grand tour he loitered in Venice and lingered in Naples, wandering to Paestum, feasting in the orange groves of Sorrento, and penetrating the Blue Grotto at Capri. In Venice the songs of the country, in Naples the barcarolles, made his memory as he came away a thicket of singing-birds. Those ever-renewed snatches and remembered refrains of songs, Venetian and Neapolitan, like a sponge passed over a Giorgione, brought out the mellow richness of Italy, and as he paced Broadway and hummed a tender melody, he walked where Vittoria Colonna had trod, and heard the faint beat of oars upon moonlit Como. One morning, hard at work in his chamber, where only the confused roar of the city was audible, a strain rose high and clear above it all, with a soft, pathetic, penetrating urgency, "So' marinaro di questa marina," and, all else forgotten, he was once more rocking on Italian waters, and the red-capped fisher-boys filled the air with song.

He ran down, and into the street, and around the block, and, lo! Signor Raffaello was the fond magician. He was turning the crank of his heavy organ, and Don Whiskerando, feathered cap in hand, was climbing the balcony of the drawing-room windows, and Signor Raffaello was raising his eyes towards the upper windows to see if haply some child or nurse attended. Eugenio dropped more than a penny into the ready hand of the signore, and was gone before the swarthy magician could make out his benefactor. Eugenio gained his room, and with sympathetic intelligence the signore, playing out the College Hornpipe, once more touched the stop of "So' marinaro," and renewed the happy spell.

It is not fine music, that of the hand-organ and the street bands; it is indeed too oft a cracked and spavined pleasure. Doubtless it is justly classified as one of the street noises, and street noises are probably nuisances to be abated. But strolling in the eastern quarters of the city, beyond the domain of the Academy and the Metropolitan Opera-house and the halls of Steinway and Chickering, have you never seen an eager and ragged little rabble happily watching Don Whiskerando, while their elders are plainly pleased for a moment with that tuneful noise? The fruit is not wholly sound, but it is far from rotten. The music is poor, but the pleasure is unquestionable. Possibly the "Gotterdammerung," and even Siegfried's "Tod," would pass these people unmarked, like the wind. They cannot hold those mighty measures. But they are receptive of these little tunes. In a life of not much enjoyment this brings them some pleasure. Shall it be stopped altogether? It is the business of these peddlers of tunes to wander. They will move on if you do not want them. But must they also move away from those who do want them?

If there be too much noise in the streets, might not some other form of noise have been first silenced than that of the street musicians? There are the factory whistles and the church-bells. For the necessity of the first something may be said. But the heavy clangor of the bells is doubtless more than a discomfort to many, and it is wholly useless, while the music of the organs and the bands is a pleasure. Do the Aldermen, like Homer, sometimes nod? Sometimes, for an inadvertent hour, do the finer instincts of public spirit flag in those civic bosoms? What evil genius, hostile to the enjoyment of the people, persuaded them? Did the city fathers for one ill-starred moment forget their Tacitus, and silence the street music unmindful of those words, so familiar to them in their hours of classic relaxation-- Solitudinem faciunt, pacem appellant?

A LITTLE DINNER WITH THACKERAY

Mr. Lester Wallack in his reminiscences speaks of Thackeray, whom he knew in New York, and recalls with admiration his simple and hearty ways. Wallack says that as he returned from acting at his father's theatre, then at the corner of Broadway and Broome Street, to his lodgings in Houston Street, he used to pass Thackeray's quarters, who was living with the late William D. Robinson in Houston Street, and if he saw a light in the window he went in, and the gentlemen finished the night together. He says that Thackeray had a boy's enjoyment of the stories that the late-comer told, and although the guest does not say it, the reader easily imagines that had he been in Thackeray's place he would have shared Thackeray's pleasure in the gayeties of his guest. Thackeray had the tastes of the town, and Charles Marlowe and My Awful Dad were sure to bring their own welcome.

Wallack also alludes to a dinner which Thackeray gave at the old Delmonico's, at the corner of Broadway and Chambers Street, at the end of his first visit to this country. He had been most warmly received, and he had given universal delight by his lectures upon the English Humorists. The charm of these lectures is evident in the reading, but the pleasure of hearing them is quite indescribable. They were delivered in Dr. Chapin's old church, upon the east side of Broadway just below Prince Street, to an exceedingly intelligent and sympathetic audience, who knew their enjoyment to be the highest kind of literary pleasure. The thorough appreciation of the men whom he described, the sweet and sinewy simplicity of his English, of which he was a twin master with Hawthorne, the constant play of his kindly humor, and manly pathos and sympathy, with his rich voice and massive, magnetic presence, his melodious and refined inflection in speaking, and his quiet, easy, colloquial manner, thrusting thumbs and forefingers in his waistcoat-pockets--all these, pleasing to the mind and sense, made him the pleasantest of lecturers, and still enchant the memory of those "happy evenings all too swiftly sped."

Just before he sailed upon his return to England he gave the dinner at Delmonico's of which Wallack speaks, to repay many civilities, and assembled a miscellaneous party of twenty or thirty guests. They were men of various distinction, "everybody being somebody," as one of the guests remarked while he glanced around the table. Thackeray was in high spirits, and when the cigars were lighted he said that there should be no speech-making, but that everybody, according to the old rule of festivity, should sing a song or tell a story. Lester Wallack's father, James Wallack, was one of the guests, and with a kind of shyness, which was unexpected but very agreeable in a veteran actor, he pleaded earnestly that he could not sing and knew no story. But with friendly persistence, which yet was not immoderate, Thackeray declared that no excuse could be allowed, because it would be a manifest injustice to every other modest man at table, and put a summary end to the hilarity. It was to be a general sacrifice, a round-table of magnanimity. "Now, Wallack," he continued, "we all know you to be a truthful man. You can, of course, since you say so, neither sing a song nor tell a story. But I tell you what you can do, and what every soul at this table knows you can do better than any living man--you can give us the great scene from the 'Rent Day.'"

There was a burst of enthusiastic agreement, and old Wallack, smiling and yielding, still sitting at the table in his evening dress, proceeded in a most effective and touching recitation from one of his most famous parts. It was curious to observe from the moment he began how completely independent of all accessories the accomplished actor was, and how perfectly he filled the part as if he had been in full action upon the stage. It is only this effect that the Easy Chair recalls, but it was not to be forgotten. No enjoyment of it was greater, and no applause sincerer than those of Thackeray, who presently sang his "Little Billee" with infinite gusto. The song and story went round, as Lester Wallack records, but the by-play of the dinner, which is often the best part of such a banquet, was different for each of the guests. The Easy Chair recalls one incident which was a striking illustration of the masterly and phenomenal assurance of a well-known figure in the Bohemian circles of New York at that time, but whom it must veil under the name of Uncle Ulysses.

By the side of the Chair sat a poet, whom also it must protect by the name of Candide, for a simpler and sincerer literary man never lived. It was in the time, as Thackeray was fond of saying, Planco Consule, which in this instance means in the time of the old Putnam's Monthly Magazine. The number for the month had been just published, and Candide had contributed to it his "Hesperides," a charming poem, although the reader will not find that title in his works. He and the Easy Chair were speaking of the magazine, when Uncle Ulysses, who had never met Candide, and knew him only by name, dropped into the chair beyond him, and at a convenient moment made some pleasant remark to the Easy Chair across Candide, who sat placidly smoking. "By-the-bye," said Uncle Ulysses presently, "what a good number of Putnam it is this month! But, my dear Easy Chair, can you tell me why it is that all our young American poets write nothing but Longfellow and water? Here in this month's Putnam there is a very pretty poem called 'Hesperides.' Very pretty, but nothing but diluted Longfellow."

This was said to the Easy Chair most unsuspiciously across the author of the poem, and the moment it was uttered, the Easy Chair, to prevent any further disaster, broke in and said, "Yes, it is a delightful poem, written by our friend Candide, who sits beside you. Pray let me introduce you. Mr. Candide, this is Uncle Ulysses."

Candide turned, evidently swelling with anger, and the Easy Chair was extremely uncertain of the event, when Uncle Ulysses, with exquisite urbanity and a look of surprise and pleasure, held out his hand, and said: "Mr. Candide, this is a pleasure which I have long anticipated. I am very much honored in making your acquaintance, and I was just speaking to the Easy Chair of your delightful poem just published in Putnam. I congratulate you with all my heart."

Candide, astonished but perplexed, and yielding to the perfect bonhomie of Uncle Ulysses, half involuntarily put out his hand, which our uncle shook warmly, and in five minutes his fascinating tongue had charmed Candide so completely that the Easy Chair is confident that the good poet always supposed that in some extraordinary manner he had misunderstood Uncle Ulysses's remark touching the imitative tendency of young American poets.

So one reminiscence produces an ever-widening ripple of reminiscences. Those which circle about the recollection of Thackeray in this country are very many, but generally unrecorded. They linger, and appear occasionally in allusions like those of Lester Wallack. But whenever they are told they pay homage to the humorist. They recall his constant, sturdy, kindly simplicity and kindliness. Wallack speaks of a certain boyish or boy-like quality in Thackeray. It was certainly there. He had the utmost sympathy with boys, and one of his gay caricatures of himself represents him at a Christmas pantomime standing with two boys behind the rest of the audience, he towering aloft and seeing everything over other people's heads, while his poor little comrades, far down about his knees, ruefully see nothing. But you know that if no other seat could be found, the good giant would soon have them upon his shoulders, and all would be boyishly happy together. "They think I am a grinning surgeon with a scalpel," said the tender-hearted man. But those who have not found and felt the heart are yet to learn to know Thackeray.

CECILIA PLAYING

As the great musical artists, especially the pianists, arrive one after the other, and lead the town captive, one asks, not whether there be any limit to the number, but to the skill. Last year there was the prodigy, the phenomenon, the boy Hofmann, and all the superlatives were spent in his praise. This year it is Rosenthal--valley of roses--and sweet as their attar is his spell. "Well, what is he?" "Simply miraculous; never was there anything like him." "But Rubinstein?" "Yes, a great genius, but he himself said that at every concert he dropped notes enough to furnish two concerts." "Then it is skill only, technique?" "Not at all; it is perfection of feeling, conception, touch, everything. Perhaps not the greatest of composers. But for playing--ah!"

Rapture is one kind of criticism. Perhaps in music, the effect of which is emotional, rapture, if you know the person, is the best criticism. The artist who can kindle to the utmost enthusiasm of delight a musically sensitive person who is also an exquisitely skilful player, and whom mere marvels of execution do not affect beyond reason, may be accepted as a very remarkable artist. Temperament also counts for much in estimating musicians. Natures are sympathetic. A silent, separate chord vibrates in response to a thrill of sound which leaves other things unmoved. The heart of the young man speaks to the psalmist, but the old man's may be dull and unawakened. The homoeopathic formula, like cures like, may be adapted to musical criticism at least so far as to say that like touches like.

When Cecilia says that she has been enchanted by the playing of any artist, the quality of her feeling and expression justly interprets the character of his performance. When Jenny Lind first sang in America one of the most accomplished critics said that he must wait a little to decide whether she was a great singer. That critic could never really hear her. Another said that she was a consummate ventriloquist. He meant that in the Herdsman's

Song and the other Volkslieder and native melodies there was an effect of vocalism which seemed to him a trick. But to others it suggested wide, solitary horizons, the sadness and seclusion of remote Northern life. Mere imagination, retorted the critics. Yes, but to what does art, especially musical art, appeal? Rubinstein, as he said of himself, dropped notes without number under the piano. Thalberg did not, nor Henri Herz. But they dropped something which Rubinstein did not. The sunshine of a December day in this latitude is often cloudless and beautiful. But it unfolds no rose and restores no leaf to the bare bough.

A sweet and true, a full-volumed and thoroughly trained voice, is a rare gift to any man. But without a certain quality in the singer it is a perfect fruit without flavor. The singing that haunts us, which becomes part of our life, which fills the memory with tender and happy images of other days and scenes, is not necessarily that of the finest voices, but of that mingling in music of voice and skill and feeling which weave an enchanted spell. Those who have known the troubadour Riccardo have doubtless heard what are called greater voices, artists who hold for a triumphant moment the hazardous peak of the high C, whose roulades and phrasing are exquisite and admirable. But the singer whom they wish to hear, whose singing is a part of life, like the beauty of flowers and the dawn, is the singing of the troubadour Riccardo. It is so with Cecilia's playing, and it is impossible to suppose a person sensitive to music who could escape its spell.

When she sits at the piano and touches the keys, they respond, as one whom she fascinated said, with such smooth sweetness that you think there is conscious pleasure to them in that pressure. It is apparently as gentle, he insisted, as that of the breeze upon the grass which lightly sways beneath it. The impression upon this sensitive youth was a test of the character of her playing. If he had said she sings with her fingers he would have said what he doubtless thought, and what is true. She plays German songs--some of the familiar songs in the collections, or something of Lassen's or Weit's, or Abt's, or one of a thousand other songs, and the playing is like exquisite singing. It fills the mind with pictures, with persons, with scenes, and with that unspeakable content which only such music can give to the lovers of music. "What on earth is it all about?" said the Senator at the Symphony Concert, "and why do people come here?" The Hottentot would have asked the same question if he had heard the Senator upon the stump.

If the fairy godmother who presides over the cradle should give the newcomer the choice of gifts, what gift more precious could the young stranger ask than the power of giving a pleasure so pure as that which Cecilia's playing imparts? It is one of her praises that if the choice had been given to her she would instantly have selected the very power which the good fairy bestowed. For in giving the pleasure she does only what she delights to do and would have chosen to do. One philosopher, speaking to the Easy Chair of another, whose serenity was as undisturbed by events as the firmament by clouds, said of himself that he subdued more devils before breakfast every day than his serene brother had encountered in his whole life. Yet the serene brother's lofty repose was not less admirable because it was a quality of temperament, and not a triumph of the will; and it is not less the merit of Cecilia that the happiness she diffuses is as involuntary as the fragrance of the sweetbrier.

What is done without effort seems not to have been taught, and it is not easy to fancy Cecilia drudging at exercises and laboring at scales. Canaries, indeed, are trained to sing, and even young birds to fly. Yet the training is but showing them how to give themselves free play. To express entire facility we say that an act is done as naturally as a bird sings. Not less naturally does Cecilia play. You listen, and the song which you knew seems to sing itself, but enveloped with a richness and fulness of flowing accompaniment which is like the harping of aerial choirs. Then with others she plays the great music, concerted Bach or Beethoven, Chopin, Schumann, or Wagner, Weber or Mendelssohn; now an old gavotte, now a quaint fantasia, and why not a toccata of Galuppi Baldassero? It is more than a hint or a reminiscence, although it is not an orchestra. But when those fingers kindred with Cecilia's sweep the keys together, the listener wonders whether the hearer of the full orchestra has caught from it the subtle and exquisite significance of the strain which has poured from those enchanted pianos.

The piano is called an inadequate instrument. Perhaps it is, until you hear Cecilia play. Then by some secret sympathy you find yourself murmuring, "Not so sweetly sang Plumer as thou sangest, mild, childlike, pastoral M----; a flute's breathing less divinely whispering than thy Arcadian melodies when, in tones worthy of Arden, thou didst chant that song sung by Amiens to the banished Duke, which proclaims the winter wind more lenient than for a man to be ungrateful!"

THE MANNERLESS SEX

To be told that the lily is not the flower of vestals, but of Venus, could not be more surprising than to be assured that the mannerless sex is not that of the troubadour Rudel, but of the Lady of Tripoli, to whom he sang. Such a suggestion is, of course, but a merry fancy. Could any critic, however inclined to misogyny, seriously allege ill-manners against the sex of Sidney's sister, Pembroke's mother? Yet this is precisely what has been recently done.

One censor enumerates and catalogues and classifies the sins against good manners of which the sex is guilty. He presents a philosophical analysis of the recondite forms of feminine discourtesy. It is the ancient sage again pitilessly exposing the Lamia. It is Circe out-Circed. He details the degrees of offence--in young women, in women who are no longer classed as girls, in nearly all women, in women with the fewest social duties. Then the boundless Sahara of ill-manners opening before him, and with a certain zest of unsparing scrutiny, he treats of the behavior of women in the horse-cars, at the railway station buying tickets, at the post-office, where the rule is imperative, first come first served, but where this chief of sinners presses for a reversal of the beneficent rule of equality in her favor.

Still more flagrant aspects of misconduct rise upon the censor's view of the sex. The shameful or shocking treatment by woman of those whom she holds to be her inferiors cries to Heaven. Her heartless detention of railway porters staggering under their burdens, her browbeating of "tradespeople," cause this observer of fine susceptibilities and an acute sense of the becoming to lament the desuetude of the ducking-stool. The more general outrage, however, apparently common to the sex from Helen of Troy to Florence Nightingale, is, according to our censor, the spite of women towards each other, which mounts into an ecstasy of rudeness when "woman goes a-shopping."

But our Cato the elder does not permit man truculently to exalt himself by contrast with discourteous woman. He expressly disclaims the declaration of the implication that man is mannerly, while woman is not. In many men he remarks indifference to rudimentary courtesies, and in many women a gentle regard for others which deserves even eulogy. The sum of the whole matter, nevertheless, is that the average woman is more neglectful of common courtesy than the average man.

"And no wonder," exclaims Cato the younger, "for the foolish fondness of man teaches her discourtesy." If man, instead of giving her his seat in the railway car, and slavishly removing his hat in the elevator, and acquiescing in her tyrannical hat at the theatre, insisted upon his legal rights in a bargain, and required the railroad company to furnish without evasion the commodity of seats for which it has been paid, or if he brought the manager to task for allowing one of his customers to steal what he has sold to another--namely, a view of the play--the world would tremble on the edge of the millennium of good manners.

This terrible arraignment is a comprehensive accusation of selfishness against the sex. But it seems to be a generalization founded on a local and restricted observation. It is true of the woman of many artists and critics. The women of Du Maurier, for instance, belong to "a set," but they are not representatives of a sex. Becky Sharp is no more a typical woman than Amelia, or Scott's Rebecca. Major Dobbin is as much a type of men as Lord Steyne. Should our social censor sequester himself for a time in any remote rural community, it would hardly occur to him to signalize the sex of the rural wives and mothers as the selfish sex. And in town, although there are a few fleeting hours of flattered youth in which the beautiful and fortunate Helen may tread on air and breathe adulation until she feels herself a goddess, yet a newer and younger Helen is always gently pushing her from the throne. Of all seasons that of blossoms is the briefest, and the maturer Helen, of whom the sex is composed, is not wayward and selfish, is no longer "uncertain, coy, and hard to please," but patient, self-sacrificing, and true.

Man was self-convicted from the beginning. Could there be more ineffable selfishness than Adam's plea in the garden? "The woman whom thou gavest to be with me, she gave me of the tree and I did eat." Had Eve been of no finer stuff than he, she would have left him there. But his craven answer at once revealed the essential weakness that demanded the devoted stay of unselfish constancy. Were woman the ever-selfish, Eve would have abandoned Adam to himself while she tripped to solitary pastures new. But the same quality that sustains the secluded farmer and his household in the hills supported the timid tiller of the first garden as the sword flamed behind him over the closing gate of Eden. If Adam plained that Eve had lost him Paradise, does not every son of Adam own that she has regained it for him?

The watchful traveller in city cars, or wherever his fate may guide, is not struck by the discourtesy of the gentler sex. The observable phenomenon in city transit is the resolute, aggressive, conscious selfishness of man hiding behind a newspaper, with an air of unconsciousness designed to deceive, or brazening it out with an uneasy aspect of defending his rights. This is the spectacle, and not a supercilious assumption on the part of the shop-girl. Her courteous refusal to take a seat, or courteous acceptance of it, is more familiar than the courteous proffer.

Cato the younger suggests that it is a wrong that seats should not be provided, and holds that the company should be compelled to furnish the accommodation for which it is paid. It is a Daniel come to judgment, but how shall it be done? Shall men keep their seats until, by sheer shame, and in deference to indignant public protest, the company does its duty? But would the shame and indignation be due to the consciousness that the accommodation paid for was not provided? Would they not arise rather from the consciousness of the peculiar wrong that the gentler sex should be so incommoded? And, if so, while the incommodation lasts, what but the selfishness of men devolves it upon women! But if men should agree to surrender their seats that women should be first accommodated, is there any doubt that the wrong would be speedily righted? And to what would this be due but to the fact that the selfishness of men would insist upon the comfort of which, while the incommodation lasts, they deprive women?

Indeed, if all men in crowded cars should resolutely keep all women standing, the wrong would not be righted, because women would submit with unselfish patience, and because corporations have no souls. The better plan, therefore, is that all men shall refuse to see a woman stand, because if men are really discomforted by their own courtesy they will compel redress.

In a world turned topsy-turvy, where Cordelia and Isabella and Juliet were mannerless, the other sex might be eulogized by distinction as mannerly. But in this world is the gentle Bayard as truly the type of the average man as Jeanie Deans of the average woman?

ROBERT BROWNING IN FLORENCE

It is more than forty years since Margaret Fuller first gave distinction to the literary notices and reviews of the New York Tribune. Miss Fuller was a woman of extraordinary scholarly attainments and intellectual independence, the friend of Emerson and of the "transcendental" leaders, and her critical papers were the best then published, and were fitly succeeded by those of her scholarly friend, George Ripley. It was her review in the Tribune of Browning's early dramas and the "Bells and Pomegranates" that introduced him to such general knowledge and appreciation among cultivated readers in this country that it is not less true of Browning than of Carlyle that he was first better known in America than at home.

It was but about four years before the publication of Miss Fuller's paper that the Boston issue of Tennyson's two volumes had delighted the youth of the time with the consciousness of the appearance of a new English poet. The eagerness and enthusiasm with which Browning was welcomed soon after were more limited in extent, but they were even more ardent, and the devoted zeal of Mr. Levi Thaxter as a Browning missionary and pioneer forecast the interest from which the Browning societies of later days have sprung. When Matthew Arnold was told in a small and remote farming village in New England that there had been a lecture upon Browning in the town the week before, he stopped in amazement, and said, "Well, that is the most surprising and significant fact I have heard in America."

It was in those early days of Browning's fame, and in the studio of the sculptor Powers, in Florence, that the youthful Easy Chair took up a visiting-card, and, reading the name Mr. Robert Browning, asked, with eager earnestness, whether it was Browning the poet. Powers turned his large, calm, lustrous eyes upon the youth, and answered, with some surprise at the warmth of the question:

"It is a young Englishman, recently married, who is here with his wife, an invalid. He often comes to the studio."

"Good Heaven!" exclaimed the youth, "it must be Browning and Elizabeth Barrett."

Powers, with the half-bewildered air of one suddenly made conscious that he had been entertaining angels unawares, said, reflectively, "I think we must have them to tea."

The youth begged to take the card which bore the poet's address, and, hastening to his room near the Piazza Novella, he wrote a note asking permission for a young American to call and pay his respects to Mr. and Mrs. Browning, but wrote it in terms which, however warm, would yet permit it to be put aside if it seemed impertinent, or if, for any reason, such a call were not desired. The next morning betimes the note was despatched, and a half-hour had not passed when there was a brisk rap at the Easy Chair's door. He opened it, and saw a young man, who briskly inquired,

"Is Mr. Easy Chair here?"

"That is my name."

"I am Robert Browning."

Browning shook hands heartily with his young American admirer, and thanked him for his note. The poet was then about thirty-five. His figure was not large, but compact, erect, and active; the face smooth, the hair dark; the aspect that of active intelligence, and of a man of the world. He was in no way eccentric, either in manner or appearance. He talked freely, with great vivacity, and delightfully, rising and walking about the room as his talk sparkled on. He heard, with evident pleasure, but with entire simplicity and manliness, of the American interest in his works and in those of Mrs. Browning, and the Easy Chair gave him a copy of Miss Fuller's paper in the Tribune.

It was a bright and, to the Easy Chair, a wonderfully happy hour. As he went, the poet said that Mrs. Browning would certainly expect to give Mr. Easy Chair a cup of tea in the evening, and with a brisk and gay good-bye, Browning was gone.

The Easy Chair blithely hied him to the Cafe Done, and ordered of the flower-girl the most perfect of nosegays, with such fervor that she smiled, and when she brought the flowers in the afternoon, said, with sympathy and meaning: "Eccola, signore! per la donna bellissima!"

It was not in the Casa Guidi that the Brownings were then living, but in an apartment in the Via della Scala, not far from the place or square most familiar to strangers in Florence--the Piazza Trinita. Through several rooms the Easy Chair passed, Browning leading the way, until at the end they entered a smaller room arranged with an air of English comfort, where, at a table, bending over a tea-urn, sat a slight lady, her long curls drooping forward. "Here," said Browning, addressing her with a tender diminutive-- "here is Mr. Easy Chair." And, as the bright eyes but wan face of the lady turned towards him, and she put out her hand, Mr. Easy Chair recalled the first words of her verse he had ever known:

"'Onora, Onora!' her mother is calling,
She sits at the lattice, and hears the dew falling,
Drop after drop from the sycamore laden
With dew as with blossom, and calls home the maiden.
'Night cometh, Onora!'"

The most kindly welcome and pleasant chat followed, Browning's gayety dashing and flashing in, with a sense of profuse and bubbling vitality, glancing at a hundred topics; and when there was some allusion to his "Sordello," he asked, quickly, with an amused smile, "Have you read it?" The Easy Chair pleaded that he had not seen it. "So much the better. Nobody understands it. Don't read it, except in the revised form, which is coming." The revised form has come long ago, and the Easy Chair has read, and probably supposes that he understands. But Thackeray used to say that he did not read Browning because he could not comprehend him, adding, ruefully, "I have no head above my eyes."

A few days later--

"O gift of God! O perfect day!"--

the Easy Chair went with Mr. and Mrs. Browning to Vallombrosa, and the one incident most clearly remembered is that of Browning's seating himself at the organ in the chapel, and playing--some Gregorian chant, perhaps, or hymn of Pergolesi's. It was enough to the enchanted eyes of his young companion that they saw him who was already a great English poet sitting at the organ where the young Milton had sat, and touching the very keys which Milton's hand had pressed.

It was midsummer in Italy, but the high, narrow streets of Florence hold a protecting shade over the lingering pilgrim, and from such companionship as that of the Via della Scala even Venice long wooed in vain. But at last, reluctantly, although the fascinating way lay through Bologna and Ferrara, the journey began towards Venice; and in that city, so early and always dear to Browning, whose romantic life and story most deeply touched and stirred his imagination, and in which he lately died, the Easy Chair received from the poet a glimpse of his earliest impressions.

Writing from Casa Guidi, in Florence, on the 9th of August, 1847--Casa Guidi, upon which a tablet records that there Elizabeth Barrett and Robert Browning lived, and "Casa Guidi Windows," "Sonnets from the Portuguese," and "Aurora Leigh" were written--Browning says:

"The people of the house there [Via della Scala] told us honestly on the morning of your departure that they could only receive us for a single month, at the expiration of which were to begin certain whitewashings and repaintings. We continued our quest, therefore, and at last found out this cool, airy apartment, which we shall occupy for another month or six weeks, whatever be our subsequent plans, for Rome, or for the Venice you describe....

"I spent a month of entire delight there some eight years ago, and tho' nothing I have since seen has effaced the impressions of my visit, yet your fresher feelings bring out whatever looks faint or dubious in them, as a gentle sponging might revive the gone glory of some old picture. (You must know I have seen an exquisite copy of a Giorgione, the original of which--so I was told--grew only visible and intelligible when thus wetted.) I am glad the railroad and gas-lighting do Venice no more wrong, and that you find all the old strange quietness, and--ought I to be glad of this, too?--depopulation; for of late years we have heard a great deal of the returning life and prosperity of the place; and Mr. Valery, I observe, retracts his earlier bodements of a speedy extinction of what little glimmer of light he still saw.

"As for me, I remember that the accounts of the depreciation of the value of houses, coupled with the indifference of the inhabitants of them, were enough to set one dreaming (in one's gondola!) of getting to be as rich as Rothschild, buying all Venice, turning out everybody, and ensconcing one's self in the Doge's palace, among the dropping gold ornaments and flakes of what was lustrous color in Titian's or Tintoret's time, waiting for the proper consummation of all things and the sea's advent.

"But do you really find the air so light and pure in this by right mephitic time of August, with those close calles, pestilential lagunes, etc., etc., and all that our informants frighten us with? Should a winter in Venice prove no more formidable in its way than it seems a summer does, why, we may have cause to regret our determination to give up our original plans. I am sure your kindness will tell us, should it be enabled, any good news of the winter and spring climate--if weak lungs may brave it with impunity."....

To this letter of Browning's, written in his young manhood--he was then thirty-five--about the Venice which always charmed him, may be well added the words of the Lady of Mura, written only a few weeks before the poet's death. Asolo is a sequestered town, which Browning said that he discovered, and in which he fell under the glamour of very Italy. In the prologue to his last volume, written in September before the letter that follows, the poet says:

"How many a year, my Asolo,
Since--one step just from sea to land--
I found you, loved, yet feared you so--
For natural objects seemed to stand
Palpably fire-clothed!"
The letter says:
"I have bought in ancient Asolo a narrow, tall tower, into which
in the last century (very early) a house was built, and this
curious place I have selected for villeggiatura when the
scirocco is too strong in Venice for health or comfort. It was
here that Browning fifty years ago was inspired to write
'Sordello' and 'Pippa Passes,' so to me it has that charm added
to many others. It is such a rough and out-of-the-way little
place that you may only know it by name. There is no hotel, no
railway, no factory, no sign of modern civilization. It is on a
hill, which has an ancient ruined fortress at the top, and was
an old Roman settlement, with the usual Roman mise en scene,
baths, amphitheatre, etc., in the days of Pliny, who somewhere
mentions it.
"Near my tower, which is built in the ancient wall of the
mediaeval town, is the tower of Caterina Cornaro, and one sees
from most of my windows, so high are they, the whole Marca
Trevigiana, with its tragic and dramatic associations of the
early Middle Ages; the Eccelini, the Azzi, the incessant wars
in which towns were treated by the tyrants like shuttlecocks in
the game of battledoor.
"Browning and his sister have been here for the last six weeks,
and you may fancy how intensely the poet enjoys revisiting
after so many years the scenes of his youthful inspirations. He
was only twenty-five or six when he first discovered Asolo....
Few young people are so gay and cheerful as he and his dear old
sister.".....
It is a pleasant last glimpse of Browning at Asolo, where the master-spell of
Italy first touched his genius, and whither at the end he came--"asolare, to
disport in the open air, amuse one's self at random"--at heart and in temper
of the same unquenched and unquenchable vitality as on that summer day
long ago when he sat where Milton had sat, and pressed, as Milton had
pressed, the keys of the organ at Vallombrosa.
"Ah, did you once see Shelley plain?
And did he stop and speak to you?
And did you speak to him again?--
How strange it seems and new!"

GEORGE WILLIAM CURTIS

PLAYERS

It is no wonder that Longfellow wrote a sonnet to Mrs. Fanny Kemble upon her Readings. Those evenings were indeed "happy," and "too swiftly sped." Mrs. Kemble's ample person draped in gold-colored silk, her flowing black hair folded and braided in some large style about her head, her rich and low and exquisitely modulated voice, her queenly presence, her magnificence of self-possession--all this fascinating personality made her reading memorable, and like a torch which reveals the perfect detail of great sculpture or architecture, her genius gave the whole value to every character and scene of the play. Did Whitfield pronounce the word Mesopotamia like a wind harp sighing exquisite music? So Mrs. Kemble's recitation of the soliloquy of Jaques left one line in the recollection of one hearer, which, like an enchanted fruit, is constantly renewing its freshness and flavor. It is one of the most familiar lines in Shakespeare,
"All the world's a stage,
And all the men and women merely players."
The Easy Chair was introduced to Mr. John Gilbert not very long before the death of that delightful actor. It was in the morning, and Mr. Gilbert was dressed with gentlemanly simplicity and propriety. But as he bowed courteously the good player seemed to have stepped aside for a moment from his real life, and to be not quite at ease when saluted by his own name rather than by that of Sir Peter, or Squire Hardcastle, or Sir Anthony Absolute. Methought, as the sages of the theatre say, that the stage was a more natural life to him. He knew the part of his own personality less familiarly than some other parts. The modest gentleman seemed half anxious to escape, as if he were caught in an undress, and pined for the security of the embroidered coat of a character.
Let us stop for a moment to say how fine he was in that embroidered coat.

115

It is hard to conceive that Mr. Gilbert can have any adequate successor in his own parts. He created the standard, and when living memory can no longer measure the comparative excellence of other performances of them, they will be tested by the traditions of Gilbert. The plain good-breeding of his Hardcastle had a rustic quality, or flavor, rather, which was delicately discriminated from the courtly refinement of his Sir Peter. There was the essential gentleman in both, but it was the country gentleman in one and the city gentleman in the other. The touch of chuckling senility in Hardcastle's pleasure with Diggory's enjoyment of his stories, and the uxorious fondness of Sir Peter, are both of a kind, but they are not the same, and you feel the difference. Neither of these characters can be dissociated from Gilbert by those who have seen him in them, and to know that they will not be seen again under the same conditions and support is to be conscious of a public loss.

Mr. Gilbert was a professional player. But since Mrs. Kemble's voice not only pronounced the words describing us all as players, but suggested to that hearer the various significance of the words, how the universality of the truth becomes more and more apparent! In all the great interests of life--religion, politics, business--we have our exits and our entrances, and, in this, unlike Gilbert, we show ourselves to each other not as the men we are, but as players. Here is Sylvanus, for instance, who may stand for us all, most amiable of men if you could happen upon him in some happy undress moment. But they are few. The poor fellow is cast for many parts, and he plays with little intermission.

One of his characters is the politician. He depicts a furious partisan, and is so lost in his part that while the man Sylvanus speaks the truth and desires it, yet in his character of politician it is not truth or fair play that he wants, but whatever tends to advance and aggrandize his party. He carefully depreciates those with whom he does not agree. He cultivates distrust of every word spoken and every deed done by the other party. Personally he likes many of his opponents. His personal relations show that he does not really think them the rascals and impostors and traitors that in his part of politician he declares them to be. It seems often to a dispassionate observer that when he accuses them as politicians of lying, cheating, and stealing, he estimates them by his knowledge of himself as a politician. He supposes that they would not hesitate to do what, without compunction, he does himself. They are all players together, and this is a kind of stage rant designed to impress the groundlings, who, after all, compose the larger part of the audience.

Sylvanus also plays the part of a religious sectary. As a private person he enjoys greatly the wit and intelligence and stored experience of life which distinguish his neighbor Eugenius. The purity and elevation of his neighbor brighten the days on which they meet, and he is always a better and a wiser man when they part. But these are his off hours, his moments of vacation. He appears on the stage as a sectary, and plays his part with resolute energy. This part again is that of a man not pursuing truth, but so occupied with maintaining his own conception of truth that he has no time to test it. It is a comedy of great humor, because Sylvanus, as a sectary, stands against all comers to protect a spring of deep and clear water, and is so engrossed in guarding the sacred wave from the least pollution that he does not find time to remark that it is not a spring at all, but a dry sand-pit.

In the incessant playing of all these parts to which his life and powers are chiefly devoted the charming personality of Sylvanus is quite lost. The man himself, divested of the stage costume and the text of his parts, is almost unknown. Others could play the politician or the sectary or the trader, but nobody could play Sylvanus. He is a modest, intelligent man, who knows that nobody can pre-empt truth or honesty or urbanity; that good men do not become bad by holding views which he may think to be wrong; and that his friends may be deceived as readily as the friends of others. These things, which he recognizes as the merest commonplaces when he is off the stage, he derides as utter nonsense when he is in the midst of a representation. Then, in the most vehement way, which is the stage tradition of the part, he shouts that everybody who would do well must run to his side, as if we were all passengers on a ship which is capsizing, but would be righted if everybody on board lost his own balance.

It is because even such men as Sylvanus take to the stage that Shakespeare, "sitting pensive and alone, above the hundred-handed play of his imagination," calls all men and women merely players. Like John Gilbert, although we do not play characters so amusing and harmless as his upon the stage, when we are not on it we seem to be a little lost, and secretly crave the theatre. It is remarked that when actors have an off night they go and sit in front at the play.

A charming comedy often arises from forgetfulness of the fact that a play is a play, and not real. One of the finest and not unfamiliar strokes of comedy in this kind is that of a seasoned veteran in the part of a politician who turns upon another veteran with whom he differs upon a question of expediency, and striking an attitude, with an air and tone worthy of the great Folair himself, or Mr. Crummies in his loftier moments, exclaims, "Apostate!" It is conceded that there has been nothing finer on the stage since Dick Turpin pointed his finger at Jonnathan Wild and sneered, impressively, "Thief!"

It is well for the peace of mind of the nervously disposed to remember that if we are all merely players, we must not take the play too seriously. A play is a simulation for entertainment, and as we look at Sylvanus and our other friends playing the politician or the sectary, we must constantly bear in mind that it is a play, and only a play. If we really thought he came hither as a man and not a sectary, for instance, it were pity of our life. If the part is played too really, let Sylvanus heed an earlier wisdom. "Let him name his name, and tell them plainly he is Snug, the joiner."

UNMUSICAL BOXES

It was a sage of the gentler sex who, after many years of experience, remarked that "men are queer!" That they are so in a positive sense no shrewd observer of mankind would deny, but that they are so comparatively or absolutely would be a very hardy assertion. If the queen of the household is of opinion that her associate majesty is very queer because he enjoys a torrid height of the mercury in the drawing-room, he holds probably a similar view of her fondness in the dining-room for what he describes as burnt beef. A hopeless bachelor who prided himself upon what he defiantly called his freedom, used to say, with an air of commiseration and extreme caution, that he supposed his married friends were probably what they called happy. But he added that he never knew any of the happy pairs to agree upon the proper warmth of a room, or the true turn of a roast, or the just amount of fresh air. Still, he said, demurely, I do not assert that their matrimonial felicity was not great.

But the axiom of the sage of the better sex, that men are queer, has been strongly confirmed by a recent decision of the authorities of the Metropolitan Opera-house in New York. That important body, producing the figures, has announced in effect that as it is clear from the accounts that the presentation of German opera is more profitable than that of Italian and French opera combined, it is evident that the public desires to hear Italian and French opera, and therefore for the present the German opera will be discontinued. This is certainly delightful proof that men are queer, and that one respected group of them by a signal display of queerness are anxious to contribute to the gayety of nations. It is a striking illustration of the superiority of man to money, and in the mad struggle for a mere material advantage, this devotion to pure art, condemning the expense, is a noble tribute to the unselfishness of human nature.

Another view has been advanced which is also interesting to the student of mankind. It is put in this way, that if the cost of the Italian and French opera should be a hundred thousand dollars in a season more than that of the German, yet it will be gladly paid by those denizens of boxes who have an insatiable desire to proceed with their intellectual cultivation by audible conversation during the performance. The argument is that these devotees of the intellect hold that nothing is lost by not hearing the Italian and French music, and that the evening can be much more profitably devoted to the stimulating conversation which takes place in an opera box.

Still another view is even more honorable to the boxes, while it does not depreciate the performance. This view holds that the operatic situation offers a choice of delights, an embarrassment of riches.

Charming and elevating as the music may be, yet still more lofty and inspiring is the conversation, and the boxes are therefore compelled to an alternative, and very naturally and properly choose their own talk to the music. The decision of the authorities may be consequently held to be designed to secure a continuation of conversation in the boxes upon the lowest terms of loss.

This cannot but be regarded by a judicious public as a wise conclusion. It is, of course, desirable that the wit and wisdom of the box chat should continue, but at the least sacrifice; and the least sacrifice seems to be considered the Italian and French opera together with a certain sum of money. Upon these lowest terms every friend of humanity will be glad to know that the colloquial delights of the boxes will be perpetuated. It is even hinted also that there will be no disposition in an unmannerly parquet to hiss the interruption of Italian and French opera. If the boxes think fit upon intellectual grounds to accompany the dying falls of French and Italian strains with a cheerful murmur of talk, the parquet will acquiesce without a sense of loss, if, indeed, upon such occasions there should be any parquet remaining.

The noble sacrifice of those public benefactors, the unmusical boxes, is still more strikingly illustrated by the fact that the Italian opera droops in other operatic countries as with us, and that not only in England, which has been the El Dorado of the artists of the Southern school, but in Italy itself, the opera of Italy has declined. The truth probably is that for some time in all musically cultivated countries Italian opera, which was a traditional fashion, was largely maintained as a social opportunity under conditions which most favored personal display and made the least intellectual demand. It supplied also to the society in the boxes at the San Carlo, the Pergola, the Scala, the Italiens, and Her Majesty's, the entertainment, in the persons of famous prima-donnas, of an extraordinary vocal performance.

The charm of that performance was undeniable. The rippling and glittering gayety of Rossini, the sweet and tender melody of Bellini, the sparkle of

Auber, the romantic pathos of Donizetti, the brilliant melodramatic strain of Verdi--none who have felt the spell will deny the enchantment. But tempora mutantur; one age with its spirit and taste succeeds another. A deeper, stronger, more earnest taste in music, a higher general cultivation, another theory of opera, have come into the house and seated themselves in the parquet, and look askance at the boxes as the Quartier St. Antoine looked upon the Faubourg St. Germain. The boxes, with the innocent ignorance of the oeil-de-boeuf, propose to maintain the old order, to stand by Bellini and Donizetti and the last half-century. It is touching and interesting. Vive l'opera italienne! Vivent les loges! So Marie Antoinette appeared in the balcony of the banqueting hall at Versailles, and so the garde du roi sprang to its feet with gallant enthusiasm, rattling its sabres and pledging the Queen. It is a heroic story, a romantic tradition.--And the Queen? And the garde du roi?

The authorities of the opera invite the city to an interesting entertainment. Nothing has seemed more natural than the precedence of German opera at a time in which the German musical genius and cultivation are dominant, and in a city in which the German audience abounds. And now, for our pleasure, Sisyphus will take a turn at the stone, and the lovely Danaides of the boxes, in the shining garments of Worth, with soft disdain of difficulty, will essay with sieves of the finest texture to bale out the ocean.

THE DINNER IN ARCADIA

The Easy Chair went up lately to the hills to enjoy the annual dinner at Arcadia. It is a summer feast which tradition assigns to some old academy in those parts, supposed to have been founded by a pastor of the village in the days before railroads, when there was no path to Arcadia except that which is still sometimes pursued. It is a winding sylvan way through woods and by singing streams and solitary farms, and as you drive slowly on you feel yourself penetrating farther and farther into a rural seclusion to which the modern world has hardly found its way, and where you might expect to surprise a peaceful community of ancient New England, as in threading the remoter recesses and heights of the Catskill you might come upon a party of Hendrik Hudson's crew.

In this loneliness of the hills the young pastor, who was in delicate health and unmarried, relieved the sombre severity of clerical life by teaching a few boys and girls. By that fond indirection he brightened with fresh air and natural music and sunshine the dry routine of his unmated days. For the cheerless solemnity of the life of the country clergy in those times it is hard to imagine. The missionaries to East London tell us that the peculiar characteristic of that vast region, swarming with human beings, is want of entertainment. The people there do not laugh. They have no diversion. There is nothing pleasant to see or to hear. It is a huge stone mill in which human life is ground up in an endless and barren monotony of hard work.

It is odd to trace any resemblance to it in a life so different; but the old-fashioned Calvinistic divine in his small country parish, revolving in an actual world of petty details, and in another world of grim theological speculation and absorption in the contemplation of death, must have seldom smiled. The young pastor was bound by no vow of celibacy, but he knew that his life must be brief, and he gladly surrounded himself with

123

children in the guise of pupils, and when he died he left a Bible to his church, a small sum for the education of heathen youth in America, some manuscript sermons to his parents, and the rest of his little property to found an academy for godly youth.

This at least is the tradition. But when Silvertongue came once to the dinner he put the story aside airily as a pleasant fiction, and averred that the annual feast was instituted simply to glorify two legendary friends of the town and enjoy them forever. This had a sound that contrasted not inaptly with the seriousness of the hills, and suggested an origin not unlike that of the feasts in the Lacedemonian worship of the Dioscuri. Still another theory which is like to grow with time associates it with the memory of two strangers of benignant aspect, who appeared suddenly in the village like the gray-haired regicide at Hadley, and aiding the towns-people not with a sword, but with a bounty, departed. They are all pleasant tales. But the earliest tradition is likely to be the truest. It was the good pastor who sowed the modest seed which has now sprung up a hundred-fold.

This year the text of the afternoon, for the dinner begins at one o'clock, was the report of the census that the town is declining in population. The guests were a company of the people of the hills. They came from a circuit of a score of miles. The dinner is served cold, and the guests feast
"In summer, when the days are long,
On dainty chicken, snow-white bread,"
and by two o'clock the blue gauze is spread over the remnants, the benches are turned so that the whole company faces the speakers, and then speech begins.

It was the verdict of the hills upon the report of the census that if the number of individuals is decreasing, the number of families is not. The ancient quiverfuls are disappearing, and the tale of children in a family is diminishing. But the general welfare of the family itself is increasing, while the marvellous facilities of communication bring all resources into the hills, and the remote little village of the old pastor is practically becoming a suburb.

If a higher general welfare prevails, what matter if the population somewhat declines? Quality is better than quantity. If, as a Senator of Massachusetts says, the people of the hills are merely descending into the valleys, who can complain if they bring with them the simple and hardy virtues which grow upon the hills like the great agricultural staples? Let the census say what it will, statistics need not frighten until they show a decadence of character as well as a decline of population. If, however, character is decaying, if the primary conditions of that fundamental life of the country are changing, a general change may be anticipated. But in Arcadia those signs do not yet appear. Whether there are more or fewer persons than there were fifty years ago, the comfort, the resources, the opportunities are constantly greater.

Undoubtedly they bring their dangers and disadvantages. But the same steady force of character that dealt with the old difficulties can deal with the new.

Perhaps the trouble lies less in the depletion of the hills than in the surfeit of the shore. The dragon of the glittering scales that threatens American youth and maidens may be rather Sybaris by the sea than Arcadia on the hills. It may be also rather the annual half-million of utter aliens that come from other lands, strange to us in everything that fosters a homogeneous national life, rather than the hundreds who come down morally as well as numerically from the uplands nearer heaven.

So in the larger academy which the young pastor unconsciously founded the various voices of suggestion, experience, and reflection spoke. It was a rural feast, an Arcadian holiday, such as the Swedish poet Tegner might have sketched in simple and melodious measure, or Grecian artists carved upon a frieze.

Then in the late and beautiful afternoon, and later in the light of the full moon, the guests dispersed, weaving the fragmentary hints of speech into completer views and purposes of patriotic life, as the children of the fairies wove the scattered shreds of gold into shining garments. Slowly over the hills by every bowery road, towards loftier Goshen and Hawley, and higher Chesterfield, and Plainfield where Byrant sang to the Water-fowl, down winding ways to Buckland and Charlemont and Zoar, eastward to Conway and Deerfield and remoter Sunderland, and all the wide valley of the Connecticut, the pilgrims wended homeward.

THE END